CW00346629

The Blue Badge Guide's
OXFORD
Quiz Book

The Blue Badge Guide's
OXFORD
Quiz Book

Alexandra Jackson

Front cover and internals: the logo is the registered trademark of the Institute of Tourist Guiding and its use is by kind permission of the Institute.

First published 2022

The History Press
97 St George's Place,
Cheltenham, Gloucestershire, GL50 3QB
www.thehistorypress.co.uk

© Alexandra Jackson, 2022

British Library Cataloguing in Publication Data.

A catalogue record for this book is available from the British Library.

ISBN 978 0 7509 9194 0

Typesetting and origination by The History Press
Printed by TJ Books Limited, Padstow, Cornwall

MIX
Paper from
responsible sources
FSC® C013056

Contents

Acknowledgements

My thanks in preparing this book go to my long-suffering family, with particular thanks and love to my husband, Philip, who has taken up the slack at home, tested out the questions and checked up on my terrible spelling and punctuation. Also to my son, Arthur, who did the illustrations, and his siblings Matilda, Benedict and Daisy who were guinea pigs for many of the questions. Thanks also to Nicola Guy and the team at The History Press who have got everything into good shape for publication, and coped admirably with the two-year delay caused by the Covid-19 pandemic. Then, even more importantly, I'd like to thank my many fellow guides, who work in Oxford and London, especially Blue Badge colleagues Mark King and Tabby Lucas, and Green Badge aficionado and guide Felicity Lewington. Without them and the advice and enthusiasm of other guides, who I don't have space to name here (but they know who they are), this quiz book would never have been written. I hope you enjoy it!

Alexandra Jackson,
Spring 2022
alexandra@alexandrajackson.info

Foreword

Beneath Oxford's dreaming spires are many high walls and imposing gateways. And there's nothing like a high wall or a closed gate – whether it's a college or a car factory, a science lab or a sports stadium – for making me wonder what's happening inside.

The answer, in Oxford's case, is history. For a small city, Oxford has an awful lot of history. A thousand years of battles and rebellions, debates and discoveries, and a fistful of firsts, from the world's first museum to the first four-minute mile. And it's still happening, every day. History is being made.

What's more, stories are being made up. Oxford has been home or inspiration to hundreds of great storytellers down the centuries. Poets. Playwrights. Novelists. Animators. Filmmakers. Songwriters. Games designers. This is where some of Britain's best-loved children's books began, often by stepping into imaginary worlds – Wonderland, Narnia, Middle Earth and Lyra's Oxford.

If you want to step inside this fascinating city, I suggest exploring with a Blue Badge guide even if, like me, you've lived here for years. But if you prefer to adventure alone, I highly recommend you bring this particular guide. Alexandra Jackson's intriguing and entertaining questions gradually reveal Oxford's secrets and will hopefully leave you, like Alice in Wonderland, feeling 'curiouser and curiouser'. Then why not come to The Story Museum and go deeper down the rabbit hole...

Kim Pickin
Founder
The Story Museum, Oxford
www.storymuseum.org.uk
February 2022

Introduction

I love asking questions. Ask anyone who knows me. It's because I want to know the answers. Really I do! When I was little, my grandmother used to set me quizzes; I've loved them ever since. Obviously, there's the challenge of seeing if you've got the right answer, but I'm hoping to provide a bit more than that in this quiz book.

So, you'll see that the questions are pretty short but the answers are longer, adding a bit more information around the subject. When I am leading tours as a guide, I am interpreting and contextualising what there is to see. So each chapter is themed a bit like a mini tour, with the questions roughly arranged in ascending difficulty. I have tried to touch on as many different aspects of this fascinating city as possible, home of two top-class universities and a lot more besides.

As for the answers, I've given what I believe to be the right answer, but – especially with dates – that's often surprisingly difficult. When dating a building, for example, do you choose when the money was raised, the date when the foundation stone was laid or when everyone moved in? So I apologise if the date I have provided is not exactly the one you had in mind. Suffice it to say, it should be close; any major errors or omissions are entirely down to me, for which I apologise.

So why a quiz book about Oxford? Well, there are several books in this series covering London, Edinburgh and Liverpool, so Oxford seemed a natural additon. Oxford is fascinating on a number of levels. It's a broadly based, pretty cosmopolitan city in its own right, not only because of the ancient University of Oxford, but also because its manufacturing base has attracted a multicultural workforce. It now also has a second exciting younger university, Oxford Brookes. Then, as so many old buildings still fulfil their original function, a place like Oxford allows one's imagination to run wild. It's possible to walk along the same lanes and go through the same entrances as people who've had a lasting impact on our world through their ideas or their actions. There is something very special about being able to do this. No need for virtual reality here!

You can easily wander around Oxford on your own, but I would (of course) encourage you to take a tour. And then (of course) I would exhort you to take a tour from a trained guide which, for me (of course), means an Institute of Tourist Guiding accredited Blue Badge tourist guide, or an ITG Green Badge tourist guide. So please consider booking a Blue Badge or Green Badge tour of Oxford. We are all fabulously knowledgeable, properly trained and delightful people (of course), and keen to help you explore this beautiful place. With a guide by your side, there will be someone to explain and interpret all the exciting things you can see. We can show you where groundbreaking events took place, as well as what's going on in Oxford today. We will enhance your experience and make you want to explore even more. To find a suitable guide, check out britainsbestguides.org or oxfordguildoftourguides.co.uk.

Most importantly, this little book is an invitation to come and enjoy Oxford in person, an all-embracing city which has been at the heart of our country physically, intellectually and spiritually for nearly a millennium. Oscar Wilde said Oxford 'still remains the most beautiful thing in England, and nowhere else are life and art so exquisitely blended, so perfectly made one'.

About the Author

And now for a bit about me. Like the Elephant's Child in Rudyard Kipling's *Just So Stories*, I am insatiably curious. So, being a Blue Badge tourist guide is a tailor-made job for me. Despite the many examinations required to get a Blue Badge, I am continuing to learn all the time, which is what makes guiding stimulating and interesting. My family know, to their cost, that, when we are out and about, if I see something I can't immediately place, we have to make a detour to check it out, or do a fast online search. Otherwise I am impossible to live with. As for Oxford, every day I'm learning about new things happening in contemporary Oxford as well as continuing to delve deeply into the archive of this amazing city.

When I was a student at St Anne's College, University of Oxford, I was not really looking properly at my surroundings, or at least not the bits I now find interesting. So when I became a Blue Badge tourist guide, it was a treat to explore a place that I thought I knew, but had so many more secrets to divulge. In my view, being a guide is more of an art than a science. Yes, you do have to have a lot of random detail at your fingertips, but there is no point knowing lots of information if you can't contextualise it. Being well informed allows you to be confident and professional and to feel you are at the top of your game, but my aim is to share my discoveries and enthusiasms with others and to allow them to use their own eyes to appreciate and enjoy their surroundings. Most importantly, I want my clients to have an interesting and enjoyable time in Oxford.

So how did I get to be a Blue Badge guide? After reading History at the University of Oxford, I worked as an investment analyst in London before becoming a financial journalist; that was storytelling of a sort, but this is much better. I took a career break to raise four children but when they were mostly off my hands, I leapt at the chance to train as a Blue Badge tourist guide, first for Central Southern England and also for London, both of which areas include Oxford. And then, just when my family thought I was done with exams, I added an Oxford City specialist Green Badge to my armoury. I'm a Windsor and Eton endorsed guide too. So you can see that although Oxford is an especial favourite, I guide a wide area. I'm often asked which is my favourite tour – I find it impossible to choose – although walking through Oxford, explaining its history to someone who has never visited before, remains a most satisfactory experience for me.

Every working day for me is stimulating and challenging. Assignments differ – as do the people, with a wide variety of backgrounds, interests and timescales. I need to be able to cope with dramatic changes of plan, whether created by the client or the site, and also deal with the dynamic of the group. Not everyone is interested in the same things. I never know where my audience may end up – a recent substantial donation to the University of Oxford was made by an American who visited only once. He went on to make a fortune which he is now sharing with the place which amazed him as a 15-year-old boy.

When I am not guiding, I enjoy sport, music, read a lot and hang out with my family and friends. Until recently I sat as a Magistrate (JP) in the Adult, Youth and Family Courts. I have two cats and, at last count, seven chickens.

1

Town

When one thinks of Oxford, the ancient University of Oxford tends to take centre stage. Oxford is a good-sized city in its own right, with a well-established motor industry, a world-class publisher, a growing high-tech business park, numerous language schools and tutorial colleges, and a second flourishing university, Oxford Brookes. Its location on the Thames, on the crossroads of ancient trading routes, was the reason why it was settled in the first place, over 1,000 years ago. This, together with good schools of all types and plenty of open spaces, makes Oxford a popular place to live and work; and the vibrancy and economic input of its youthful population create a lively atmosphere. So most visitors should find their needs met, be they ancient or modern. There is scope for exploring, especially on foot, or, for those with less stamina, there is plenty to enjoy if you just want to stop and stare.

1. Which iconic car is assembled in Oxford?

   a) BMW 3 Series
   b) Mini
   c) Land Rover Discovery
   d) Fiat 500

2. Which international charity was founded in Oxford in 1942?

3. How many people lived in Oxford at the last (2011) census?

   a) 85,000
   b) 155,000
   c) 180,000
   d) 115,000

4. Name the newest railway station serving Oxford.

5. Which area of Oxford was built to house workers at the University Press?

6. Which green space in Oxford escaped having a ring road through it?

7. What was previously on the site of the Malmaison Hotel (opened in 2005)?

8. Why is Turl Street so called?

9. What are the Carfax Quarterboys?

10. Which four of these European cities are twinned with Oxford?

    a) Heidelberg
    b) Bologna
    c) Grenoble
    d) Thessaloniki
    e) Perm
    f) Bonn
    g) Leiden

Chapter 1 Answers

1. **b) Mini.** Car manufacture in Oxford dates back to Morris Motors, set up by William Morris, Lord Nuffield, in the early twentieth century. There have been many changes to the industry since then, with German BMW now manufacturing Minis on the Cowley site. Before World War One, Morris started repairing bicycles in his parents' back garden and then moved to Longwall Street. A generous philanthropist, Lord Nuffield gave away over £30 million, founding a college and several medical establishments.

2. **Oxfam** was set up in 1942 at the University Church of St Mary by local businessman Cecil Jackson-Cole, and others, who were concerned about famine in Greece following its occupation by Axis powers during World War Two. The first Oxfam shop, selling second-hand clothes, opened on Broad Street in 1948.

3. **b) 155,000.** With two universities in the town, it's not surprising that a third of Oxford's population is aged between 18 and 24; that's the highest proportion of young people of any place in the country. Oxford has been a popular place to live for over 1,000 years as it's in the centre of the country, and on a crossing point on the River Thames.

4. **Oxford Parkway** opened in 2015, proving a good alternative to the central station due to its proximity to

North Oxford and its generous parking provision. Running from London Marylebone, the line also serves popular Bicester Village shopping outlet. The arrival of the railway to Oxford in the 1840s was delayed to protect undergraduates from being lured to the fleshpots of London. Now many students use the Oxford Tube, which is a price-effective twenty-four-hour London coach service.

5. **Jericho.** This grid of terraced houses has been mostly gentrified. Its popularity is helped by being near the city centre and close to the canal, and the green space of Port Meadow. Workers from the nearby Eagle Ironworks also lived in this area.

6. **Christ Church Meadow**. It was given in 1354 to St Frideswide's Nunnery by Lady Montacute, whose shrine is in Christ Church Cathedral. Luckily, the proposal to run a ring road through open land was turned down in the late 1960s, allowing us to enjoy this amenity today.

7. **A prison**. An eleventh-century castle was erected on this site by Robert D'Oilly, a supporter of William the Conqueror. It was one of a trio of castles, including Windsor and Wallingford, built to suppress a local rebellion after the 1066 Norman Conquest. It then became a prison which continued to operate until 1996.

8. **Turl may come from the word 'turn' or the word 'twirl' or the word 'thirl' (narrow passage or hole).** All these refer to a turnstile in the city wall throughout the seventeenth and eighteenth centuries. This allowed pedestrian access but restricted animals and carts from entering the city at this point.

9. **They are the figures in Norman dress which chime on the quarter hour ninety-six times a day from Carfax Tower Clock, the remains of St Martin's Church.** The name Carfax comes from the Latin *quadrifurcus* via the French *carrefour*, both of which mean 'crossroads'. This junction is at the centre of Oxford. Climb ninety-nine steps up a spiral staircase to get a great view of the city.

10. c) Grenoble (1989) (one of France's oldest universities); e) Perm (1995) (linked to both Oxford University and Oxford Brookes); f) Bonn (1947) (post-war link); g) Leiden (1946) (Netherlands' oldest university). These are not the only towns twinned with Oxford.

Words, Words, Words

Oxford is not alone in having a jargon of its own, although the university has developed an especially elusive vocabulary. So, before we continue on our inquisitorial tour of Oxford, it might be helpful to avoid confusion by sorting out some local expressions.

1. What are academics normally known as (you may choose more than one)?

    a) Chaps
    b) Masters
    c) Fellows
    d) Dons

2. In Cambridge it is a 'court'; what is it in Oxford?

    a) a punt
    b) a quad
    c) a yard
    d) a hall

3. What would a University of Oxford student mean by the 'Other Place'?

    a) London
    b) Cambridge
    c) Oxford Brookes University
    d) Harvard

4. What are Oxford Bags?

   a) Boots
   b) Suitcases
   c) Trousers
   d) Jackets

5. Who typically cleans the students' rooms in an Oxford college?

   a) a mate
   b) a scout
   c) a guide
   d) a bedder

6. It's now possible to stay on a B&B basis at many Oxford colleges. What might you lay your head on overnight?

7. What is a 'gaudy'?

   a) a college reunion
   b) a gown worn at formal dinners
   c) a cake served at graduation ceremonies
   d) a rugby shirt worn for inter-college matches

8. What would you expect to wear if you were told the required dress was Sub Fusc?

9. If a University of Oxford student told you they were preparing for a collection, what would you understand by that?

   a) a lift home at the end of term
   b) a revision exam on the previous term's work
   c) a drop-off opportunity for books from the library
   d) a laundry pick-up

10. Which of the following sentences includes an Oxford comma?

a) He bought apples, oranges and bananas
b) Would you like tea, hot chocolate, or coffee?
c) He bought apples, oranges, and bananas
d) Would you like tea, hot chocolate or coffee?

Chapter 2 Answers

1. c) and d). A don, a shortening of the Latin *Dominus* or 'Master', is an academic – as is a Fellow, although a Fellow is a senior member of a college with relevant responsibilities. Both pursue their own academic interests whilst also teaching undergraduates and supervising postgraduates. They select the students for admission to the college. Just to confuse you further, at Christ Church, the Fellows are known as Students with a capital 'S', as opposed to undergraduates who, as elsewhere, are known either as students with a small 's' or as undergraduates.

2. b) A quad. Oxford (and Cambridge) colleges are typically built around an open rectangle, or several interconnected spaces with buildings with key functions provided, such as dining, reading, studying and worshipping. There is normally restricted access from the road via a gatehouse. An early example of this is Merton College's Mob Quad. Merton was the first college to achieve self-governing status in 1264 and its layout became the template for later establishments including Cambridge's oldest College, Peterhouse.

3. b) Cambridge. There is evidence of scholars gathering in Oxford in the late eleventh century. A similar community was established in Cambridge not long after as, in 1209, a group of students from Oxford decided to move to a more remote location as they disliked the friction between the town and the

university in Oxford. This explains why many of the traditions and structures of the two universities are similar.

4. c) **Trousers.** Very straight but loosely fitted with turn-ups and worn by young men in the 1920s and '30s.

5. b) **A scout (in Cambridge, it's a bedder).** Nowadays, a scout merely cleans the student's bedroom. In the past, they were more like a valet or manservant. At Christ Church, there are memorials to several college servants, recognising the important roles played by college staff in supporting many generations of students.

6. **An Oxford pillowcase.** This has a border extending beyond the main body of the pillow. As university terms are only eight weeks long, many colleges now use their accommodation for conferences or tourism.

7. a) **A college reunion,** from the Latin *gaudeamus* or 'let us rejoice'.

8. **Black suit with white shirt and white bow tie or equivalent.** Also an academic gown, which may be longer if the student is a scholar. This is what Oxford University students wear for public examinations or for other formal university occasions such as matriculation (when you start your degree) or graduation. In a 2015 vote, 80 per cent of Oxford students chose to uphold this tradition. In Cambridge there is now no longer such a dress code.

9. b) A revision exam. Oxford typically examines its students in a straightforward traditional format with little continual assessment or longer prepared pieces of work, although extended essays and mini theses are now sometimes included. Weekly work, discussed with a tutor often on a one-to-one basis, may not be marked as such but merely commented on, so termly collections help a student keep abreast of the required standard.

10. b) and c). An Oxford comma is used as the penultimate punctuation mark in a list of three or more items after 'and' and 'or'. It is a house style favoured by the Oxford University Press.

3

Gown

Ever since the small settlement on a crossing point of the Thames became a focus for learning, thus attracting a large number of opinionated young men, there has been friction between the university, or 'Gown', and the City of Oxford, or 'Town'. Indeed, it was because of this friction that a group of students broke away in the early thirteenth century and travelled east to set up a similar academic community in Cambridge.

1. Where was university business conducted in fourteenth-century Oxford?

2. Match the people to their subjects studied whilst at Oxford University:

a) Theresa May
b) Boris Johnson
c) Rowan Atkinson
d) William Golding
e) J.R.R. Tolkien
f) C.S. Lewis
g) Stephen Hawking
h) David Cameron

i) Politics, Philosophy & Economics
ii) Physics
iii) Geography
iv) Greats (Latin & Greek)
v) Electrical Engineering
vi) Greats/English
vii) Natural Science/ English
viii) Greats/English

3. Name the newspaper published weekly by students.

4. What annual ceremony at Oxford University awards honorary degrees?

5. When were academics first allowed to marry?

   a) 1909
   b) 1865
   c) 1877
   d) 1832

6. Where could undergraduates traditionally buy pith helmets?

7. Who was the first female Vice-Chancellor of Oxford University?

8. Where can you study Business at Oxford University?

9. Who recently made the largest donation to the University of Oxford since the sixteenth century?

10. Which organisation earned much of its early income from Bibles?

Chapter 3 Answers

1. In the University Church of St Mary the Virgin on the High Street by Radcliffe Square. Scholars from as early as the twelfth century met to make decisions in a church on this site, which in time included a library and a space for conferring degrees. The tower on the existing church dates back to 1270 with the spire added in 1320. The main body of the church was rebuilt in stages during the fifteenth and sixteenth centuries. For those with a head for heights, climb the 127 tower steps to enjoy a fabulous bird's-eye view of Oxford's closely packed central colleges and libraries.

2. a) iii; b) iv; c) v; d) vii; e) vi; f) viii; g) ii; h) i.

3. *Cherwell*. Named after a tributary of the Thames which runs through Oxford, this newspaper has trained many well-known journalists. It's circulated weekly in term time to 15,000 undergraduates, academics and staff and is also online. Another printed newspaper, *The Oxford Student*, is also widely read, and in 2020, The Oxford Blue, an online offering for students was launched.

4. Encaenia. A handful of invited distinguished candidates take part in a spectacular procession with university officers and academics in full regalia. This ends with a ceremony in the Sheldonian Theatre, built by Sir Christopher Wren in 1669 and modelled on the Theatre of Marcellus in Rome. Despite

having been an Oxford graduate, Lady Thatcher, British Prime Minister from 1979 to 1990, never enjoyed this honour.

5. c) 1877. Although wealthy tradesmen made up some of North Oxford's earliest residents, the main expansion followed the decision to allow Fellows to marry, as college accommodation was not suitable for families. Now, because of house price inflation, few of these properties are lived in by academics.

6. This crucial part of colonial headgear could be purchased at Ede & Ravenscroft on the High Street. Oxford, and its counterpart Cambridge, educated many young men for the overseas colonial service. A weather vane of an elephant on top of the Martin School on Broad Street dates back to the building's original purpose as The Indian Institute which was where some of this colonial training took place. Ede & Ravenscroft was set up in London in 1689. Amongst other items of formal dress it provides distinctive dinner jackets for the notorious Bullingdon Club, whose meetings have been banned from the City of Oxford due to rowdy behaviour. Members captured in a well-known 1987 photograph include two future British Prime Ministers, David Cameron and Boris Johnson.

7. Professor Louise Richardson (b. 1958) became, in effect, CEO of the university in 2016. A political scientist, 'previously at St Andrew's University in Scotland, specialises in terrorism, and is an alumna of Trinity College Dublin, UCLA and Harvard University. She will step down as Vice Chancellor in December 2022.
The position of Chancellor of the University of Oxford dates back to 1215. It is, at the time of writing, held by Lord Patten

of Barnes, the last Governor of Hong Kong (1992–97) and a history student at Balliol in the early 1960s. The Chancellor is elected by Oxford MAs (Masters of Art). Getting an MA from Oxford involves paying a modest sum seven years after matriculation, but no additional study.

8. The Saïd Business School, 2001, endowed by Syrian/Saudi billionaire Wafic Saïd. This Dixon Jones-designed building includes an open-air amphitheatre, a cloister and a ziggurat (tower) similar to Hawksmoor's 1711 St George's Church, Bloomsbury, itself modelled on the tomb of Mausolus at Halicarnassus. Oxford University was late in providing such courses for undergraduate study, only recently adding Economics & Management to Politics, Philosophy & Economics or PPE (Modern Greats), first offered in 1920.

9. Stephen Schwarzman gave £150 million in 2019 for a humanities centre to explore the ethical implications of artificial intelligence. The building will include exhibition space, a 500-seat concert hall and a 250-seat auditorium. Schwarzman made his fortune at Blackstone, a US private equity group. He was impressed by the beauty and the ancient character of the buildings as a visiting 15-year-old. Oxford, like all educational establishments, is heavily dependent on donations to enable it to remain at the cutting edge of twenty-first-century education.

10. The Oxford University Press (OUP) was established in its current format in 1668, following the 1633 Great Charter secured from Charles I by Archbishop Laud, whilst Chancellor of the University of Oxford. This entitled the university to print 'all manner of books'. OUP is a department of the University of Oxford and is overseen by fifteen delegates who are academics. For the first two centuries of its existence, OUP earned significant income from publishing the King James Bible, an English translation of the Christian Bible begun in 1604 and completed by 1611 under the sponsorship of King James I. OUP is the largest academic publisher in the world with over fifty overseas offices. Most of the actual printing of books has been outsourced since 1989, with the last vestiges of printing taking place near Oxford ending in June 2021.

4

Many Houses

Visitors to Oxford sometimes get very frustrated that they cannot find 'the university' and, to make matters worse, there is confusion as to what a 'college' might be. In Britain, a 'school' educates 5- to 18-year-olds, whilst a university, or college, is for older students. Just to confuse people further, some private schools are called colleges, e.g. Eton College. But some universities – Oxford, Cambridge and also Durham, for example – also include colleges. At Oxford and Cambridge, these colleges provide board, lodging and teaching to students and, historically, some religious provision. So, although Oxford University does provide lectures and examinations, it's not really possible, however hard you try, to see the 'university' as such. If you're now not impossibly confused, here are some questions about Oxford's colleges.

1. When did the last college in Oxford cease to be single sex?

    a) 1920
    b) 1974
    c) 2002
    d) 2008

2. Which Oxford college is widely accepted to be the first
    with self-governing status?

    a) Merton
    b) University College
    c) Balliol College

3. Which college has its own picture gallery?

4. What is the name of the newest college in Oxford?

5. How many times does Great Tom toll every evening?

6. Which college owes its existence to breakfast preferences?

7. Where could a mature student study at the University
    of Oxford?

8. Match the head of the college to the title given:

    a) St John's College   i)   Master
    b) Wadham College   ii) Dean
    c) Christ Church   iii) President
    d) Jesus College   iv) Provost
    e) Pembroke College   v)   Warden
    f) Oriel College   vi) Rector
    g) Lincoln College   vii) Principal

9. Which Oxford college was founded by public
    subscription?

10. How many colleges have similar names in both Oxford
    and Cambridge?

Chapter 4 Answers

1. d) St Hilda's College became co-educational in 2008. This was the last bastion of women-only education in Oxford. In the college's early years, when undergraduates were nicknamed Hildebeasts, there was much debate as to whether a woman could be both beautiful and intelligent. Of the four other women's colleges, St Anne's and Lady Margaret Hall admitted men in 1979, St Hugh's in 1986 and Somerville in 1994. Five men's colleges admitted women in 1974, with the rest following over the next ten years.

2. a) Merton (1264). For many years, University College claimed to be the oldest, perhaps even dating back to 872 and King Alfred. However, Merton was the first college to organise itself as a self-governing academic community, regulated by statutes and funded by endowments. This legal structure was physically formalised with a Hall, a Chapel and a gatehouse. Mob Quad, the oldest surviving quadrangle in Oxford, was completed in 1304.

3. Christ Church. The core of the collection was given by seventeenth-century alumnus John Guise. The 2,000 drawings include works by Leonardo da Vinci, Michelangelo and Raphael, and there are about 200 paintings, mostly from the Renaissance.

4. **Reuben College**. Founded as Parks College in 2019, but since June 2020 known as Reuben College, this graduate-only college admitted its first graduates in 2021. This brings the total of graduate-only colleges to eight, with thirty colleges for graduates and undergraduates, six religiously affiliated Permanent Private Halls and one college, All Souls, which admits neither graduates nor undergraduates.

5. **101 times at 9.05 p.m.** This bell, previously in now long-gone Osney Abbey, is rung every evening at five minutes after 9 p.m. GMT. This is because 9.05 p.m. GMT is in reality 9 p.m. in Oxford because it is 1.25 degrees west of the Greenwich meridian in London. This would have been the standard time in Oxford before the arrival of the railway in the 1840s which created the need to standardise times. Services at Christ Church Cathedral still start five minutes 'late', indicating Oxford's continued refusal to submit to another time zone.

6. **This college was founded in 1990 as Rewley House, achieving collegiate status in 1994 when it was renamed Kellogg College**. The college grew from a university department supporting Oxford graduates wishing to continue their education. It was endowed by the Kellogg Foundation, whose founders John Harvey Kellogg and Will Keith Kellogg first invented the cornflake in 1894 as a suitable food for residents at a Seventh Day Adventist Sanatorium.

7. **Harris Manchester College** obtained its charter in 1996, but dates back to 1757. Applicants must be over 21 years of age. A recent undergraduate is distinguished lawyer Sir Oliver Popplewell (b. 1927), who, after his retirement from the High Court, came to Harris Manchester in 2003, aged 76, to study PPE (Politics, Philosophy and Economics).

8. a) iii; b) v; c) ii; d) vii; e) i; f) iv; g) vi.

9. **Keble College** was paid for by public subscription in memory of John Keble (1792–1866), a key member of the Oxford Movement which promoted High Anglicanism and a closer association with the theology of the Roman Catholic Church. Keble was an undergraduate at Corpus Christi College and, once ordained together with John Henry Newman and Edmund Pusey, was a popular and regular preacher at the University Church. It was from their sermons known as 'tracts' that Tractarianism takes its name. Newman, however, subsequently converted to Roman Catholicism in 1845, and in October 2019 was confirmed as a saint by Pope Francis. Keble College was designed by William Butterfield in the Victorian Gothic red-brick style. Student accommodation is along corridors instead of staircases. Its dining room is very slightly larger than that of Christ Church, which is not a coincidence.

10. There is not really a precise answer to this question, as it depends on how rigid you are going to be! For starters, there are six colleges that share names: St Julin's, Wolfson, Corpus Christi, Jesus, Pembroke and Trinity. But how would you categorise Magdalen College, Oxford and Magdalene College, Cambridge, which is spelt with an additional 'e', and Queens' College Cambridge (note the apostrophe) which was founded by two queens, as opposed to The Queen's College, Oxford, which was founded by one queen, Philippa of Hainault, consort of Edward III? And then there is St Catherine's Oxford which has an 'e' in the middle whilst St Catharine's Cambridge has an 'a', and finally St Edmund Hall, Oxford, and St Edmund College, Cambridge.

5

Dreaming Spires

Let's continue to explore Oxford and the myriad of fabulous closely packed buildings. Don't be shy when you are discovering Oxford on foot (and that's the best way to do it) to stop and look more closely even at the smallest and most insignificant detail. It too deserves your attention. Imagine all those who have walked this way before you and the thoughts they had in their heads. One was poet Matthew Arnold (1822–1888); here's his description of Oxford in his elegiac 1865 poem, 'Thyrsis':

> and that sweet city with her dreaming spires,
> she needs not June for beauty's heightening,
> lovely all times she lies, lovely tonight!

There are plenty of new buildings around too, particularly within the colleges as they work hard to provide up-to-date accommodation and learning spaces for students and others. Attractive purpose-built buildings are valuable resources, when students are not in residence, for conferences, outreach programmes and summer schools. It's easy to be offhand when there is so much choice, but I've selected a cross-section for this quiz.

1. Which building in Oxford was recreated to make the dining hall at Hogwarts School of Witchcraft and Wizardry?

2. Which famous architect's early work can be seen from Broad Street?

3. Which bridge in Oxford makes you think of Venice?

4. Which architect is responsible for the Gothic revival debating chamber, now the library, at the Oxford Union Society?

5. Who never saw the college she endowed?

6. Which lakeside building was shortlisted for the 2018 Stirling Prize?

7. Which ecclesiastical architect was responsible for the Victorian chapel at Exeter College?

8. What was revolutionary about the design of St Catherine's College?

9. Which Athenian building was reproduced in Oxford?

10. Match the architect to the building:

a) Arne Jacobsen
b) T.G. Jackson
c) Rick Mather
d) William Butterfield
e) James Gibbs
f) Herzog & de Meuron
g) Zaha Hadid
h) James Stirling

i) Bridge of Sighs
ii) St Catherine's College
iii) Blavatnik School of Government
iv) Florey Building
v) Ashmolean Museum remodelling
vi) Balliol College Chapel
vii) Radcliffe Camera
viii) St Antony's Middle East Centre

Chapter 5 Answers

1. **The Hall at Christ Church** was built in 1525 as the centre of Cardinal Wolsey's grand plan for a college to be founded in his memory. It was incomplete when he fell from favour in 1530, having failed to broker a divorce for Henry VIII from his first wife, Catherine of Aragon. The hall was core to the eventual 1546 foundation of Christ Church by King Henry VIII. It has been recreated at the Warner Brothers Studios in Hertfordshire as Hogwarts School's dining hall. The staircase, with a beautiful lierne fan-vaulted ceiling, and nearby cloister also appear in the *Harry Potter* films. There are also references in the dining hall to the *Alice in Wonderland* stories (1865) by Lewis Carroll (aka Charles Dodgson) about a young girl's fantastical adventures. They were written for the children of the College's Dean, Henry Liddell, one of whom was called Alice.

2. One of **Sir Christopher Wren's** earliest works, the Sheldonian Theatre, 1669, was modelled on the Theatre of Marcellus in Rome. To achieve the 70ft roof span, Wren hid structural diagonal struts behind a painted ceiling. This building is used for matriculation (when you join the university) and graduation ceremonies, and also for Encaenia, the annual ceremony during which honorary degrees are awarded. When this building was first completed, it was also the home of Oxford University Press, although by 1715 this had moved to the newly constructed Clarendon Building nearby. The Press moved to Walton Street in 1828.

3. The bridge, which links parts of Hertford College at the junction of Catte Street and New College Lane, is known as the **Bridge of Sighs**. This is because it was thought to be like a bridge of that name in Venice in the Doge's Palace, over which condemned and 'sighing' prisoners were led to their deaths. In fact, this 1914 structure by T.G. Jackson is much more similar to the Rialto Bridge, also in Venice. Jackson was also responsible for the Examination Schools on the High Street.

4. **Anglo-Irish architect Benjamin Woodward.** Decorated by William Morris, Edward Burne-Jones and Dante Gabriel Rossetti in 1857. Woodward and Deane were also the principal architects of the 1860 Museum of Natural History in Oxford.

5. **Dorothy Wadham.** In 1610, work started on a college with money left by Nicholas Wadham. The project, completed by 1615, was supervised by his widow, Dorothy, who never visited. Alumni include Sir Christopher Wren, who met here with others during the 1650s under the warden, John Wilkins, who was very forward-thinking and promoted plans to send a man to the moon. In 1660, the group – which also included Robert Boyle and Robert Hooke, and by that time was based in London – formed the Royal Society in London, which remains a pioneering scientific institution. Wilkins married Lord Protector Oliver Cromwell's sister, Robina.

6. **Sultan Nazrin Shah Centre**, named after a Malaysian-born Worcester alumnus. It is an excellent new resource for Worcester, both for in-college activities and for external conferences and events.

7. George Gilbert Scott drew heavily on the Parisian Gothic masterpiece, Sainte Chapelle, with its flèche tower. The chapel, visible from Broad Street, was consecrated in 1868.

8. Danish architect Arne Jacobsen opened out the traditional college plan with wide spaces and gardens replacing closed quadrangles, but he also designed all the furniture and tableware to be used in the space he created in his 1962 project. The building has now been awarded Grade I listed status, thus protecting this modernist building and its contents. St Catherine's is one of the largest colleges in the university with nearly 1,000 graduates and undergraduates.

9. The Tower of the Winds. The Horologion, c.100 BC, including carvings of the eight winds, was copied by James Wyatt in 1792 for his Observatory near the old Radcliffe Infirmary. The building is now part of Green Templeton College.

10. a) ii; b) i; c) v; d) vi; e) vii; f) iii; g) viii; h) iv.

6

Mythical Beasts and Other Creatures

Oxford is full of animals, real and imagined. They are visible all around the town in carvings, street names, literature, paintings, and there are a few real-life ones too. Before most people could read and write, signs were the best way to find your way around, so pubs and inns were frequently named after animals.

1. Which children's books and allegories of Christianity feature a lion?

2. Which animals are shown on Oxford City's coat of arms?

3. Who is Lyra Bellaqua's daemon?

4. Name the lane running off the High Street named after a familiar British bird.

5. Which college has its own deer park?

6. Which bird, symbol of a sixteenth-century bishop, can be found in the front quadrangle of Corpus Christi College?

7. Where in Oxford is there a cinema named after a mythical bird?

8. Name a dog who takes a trip along the Thames?

9. Which estate on the outskirts of Oxford is named after a common British bird?

10. What fish caused havoc with Oxford City planners?

Chapter 6 Answers

1. The *Chronicles of Narnia*, a series of novels for children, by C.S. Lewis. The first book, *The Lion, the Witch and the Wardrobe*, was published in 1950 and focuses on a lion called Aslan, said to represent Jesus. Lewis was an English Literature scholar at the University of Oxford who wrote extensively and accessibly on theology following his own unexpected conversion to Christianity in 1929. Lewis and his close friend, J.R.R. Tolkien, also a member of the English faculty and author of *The Lord of the Rings* and *The Hobbit*, formed a group called The Inklings. They read their stories to each other at pubs around the town, the Eagle & Child (or 'bird and baby', as some call it) being one of their favourites, another being The Lamb and Flag. The freehold of the latter is owned by St John's College who until recently also managed the premises. Following a period of closure, it is to be relaunched by a community group appropriately calling themselves the Inklings.

2. An **ox** crossing the water is surmounted by a crowned **lion** holding a Tudor rose. They are supported by an **elephant** and a **beaver** which are linked to the local sixteenth-century Knollys and Norreys families. The city motto is *Fortis est Veritas* (Truth is Strong).

3. **Pantalaimon.** Lyra is the heroine of Philip Pullman's (b. 1946) *His Dark Materials* fantasy stories set in two

parallel universes, both of which include a recognisable Oxford. In Lyra's world each child has an ever-changing creature or daemon, which is an outward manifestation of their inner soul. At puberty, these creatures become fixed. Pantalaimon's range of forms includes a moth, an ermine, a wildcat and a mouse. When Lyra turns 12, Pantalaimon, who is a wise and steady foil to Lyra's more impulsive and passionate nature, settles as a pine marten. A further two books, *La Belle Sauvage* and *The Secret Commonwealth*, also feature Lyra. The stories have been made into a film, several plays and a television series.

4. **Magpie Lane**. This quaint shortcut, from the High Street down to Merton and Corpus Christi Colleges, was once frequented by women of the town, who provided various services to local men and, at one time, had an entirely unrepeatable name which referred to this activity. Halfway along this lane is the University College accommodation allocated in 1968 to a young Rhodes Scholar, William Clinton, later 42nd President of the United States of America. His daughter, Chelsea, lived in the same building whilst pursuing postgraduate studies.

5. **Magdalen College**, founded by Bishop William Waynflete, Bishop of Winchester, in 1458. Probably the only educational institution still to enjoy its own venison. A young T.E. Lawrence (of Arabia) apparently accepted a bet to move the deer from Magdalen to the quad in All Souls College nearby. I'd recommend strolling along Addison's Walk by the River Cherwell on this 100-acre site.

6. **The pelican of Bishop Richard Fox**. This represents Christ's self-sacrifice as it was thought that pelicans pecked their own breasts to feed their young when, in fact, they were reaching down their gullets to retrieve previously consumed fish. The pelican on the top of the sundial is a copy of Turnbull's 1581 original, and is the work of local sculptor Michael Black (1919-2019). Black also sculpted the newest version of the monumental heads outside the Sheldonian Theatre overlooking Broad Street

7. **The Phoenix in Walton Street**. This mythical bird is associated with the sun. It ends its life by self-combusting but is then recreated from its ashes. There has been a

cinema on this site since 1913. By the 1970s it had become a popular arthouse cinema. It is now owned by Cineworld.

8. **Montmorency, a fox terrier**, accompanies his master and two others in Jerome K. Jerome's Victorian classic *Three Men in a Boat (To Say Nothing of the Dog)*, which describes an accident-prone trip on the River Thames. Montmorency gets into eleven fights with local dogs on their first day in Oxford, and fourteen on the second. There is a carving of the three men and Montmorency on the west end of the Bodleian Library opposite the Sheldonian. It, and other grotesques nearby, were designed by local schoolchildren.

9. **The Blackbird Leys estate**. Houses were built here from the 1950s onwards to accommodate workers from the expanding Cowley car plants. This area of Oxford has not enjoyed the same level of prosperity as other parts of the city but has a strong community spirit.

10. **A 25ft fibreglass shark** was installed by American-born journalist and Oxford alumnus Bill Heine (1945–2019), 'crashing' into the roof of his terraced house in Headington. After a lengthy battle with the local planning authority, it was allowed to remain.

7

The Great Outdoors

More than 50 per cent of the land in the City of Oxford is open space; half belonging to the thirty-nine colleges and six private halls which make up the University of Oxford, and the remainder freely accessible to members of the public. This amount of open space makes Oxford a particularly pleasant place to explore on foot or by water.

1. What is the alternative name of the River Thames as it runs through Oxford?

   a) The Isis
   b) The Cherwell
   c) The Avon
   d) The Tamara

2. Where in Oxford can you see pineapples and bananas growing?

3. Which Oxford college has a lake in its grounds?

   a) Christ Church
   b) Magdalen
   c) Worcester
   d) Trinity

4. Where in Oxford might you see Longhorn cattle?

5. Which open space in north-west Oxford has never been ploughed?

6. Which college is obliged to maintain Oxford's medieval city walls?

7. Where were the trees mourned in a poem by Gerard Manley Hopkins?

8. Where near Oxford is there an arboretum?

9. Where near Oxford, in the mid-twentieth century, could young women receive horticultural training?

10. Which current head of state is an expert on the Upper Thames in the eighteenth century?

Chapter 7 Answers

1. a) The Isis. The origin of the name of the 215-mile-long River Thames, often said to embody liquid history, is the subject of great discussion and draws on Celtic, Roman, Egyptian and Sanskrit references. The section running from its source to Dorchester has been known as Isis since at least the fourteenth century and, as such, may have been introduced by students evoking the Egyptian mother goddess Isis, as a potential protector of the University of Oxford.

2. The greenhouses in the Oxford Botanic Garden and Arboretum. These gardens are the oldest in the country, having been set up in 1621 on the site of the medieval Jewish cemetery by Lord Danby to provide medicinal plants. The gardens beside the River Cherwell still include specimen plants.

3. c) Worcester College. Founded in 1714, it is on the grounds of an earlier monastic foundation, Gloucester College, which was dissolved in the sixteenth century. Worcester enjoys 26 acres of grounds. The buildings are primarily neo-classical, although some medieval cottages remain, as funds were not available to complete the original plans. It has a very elaborately decorated chapel.

4. Christ Church Meadow. These rare breed cattle have been reintroduced onto this ancient meadow which was given to St Frideswide's Priory in 1354 by Lady Montacute, in

exchange for a chantry for Masses to be said for her soul in what is now Christ Church Cathedral. The cattle are financed by Christ Church alumni and managed by a local farmer. Beef from this herd is, on occasion, served at high table in Christ Church.

5. **Port Meadow.** Freemen and commoners of nearby Wolvercote have grazing rights for ponies and cattle on this 440-acre piece of land which shows evidence of human use going back 2,000 years. At certain times of year (this meadow has a tendency to flood) it's possible to walk from the Trout Inn at Wolvercote to The Perch at Binsey.

6. **New College**. Every three years, this boundary is inspected to check that the college is keeping its promise to maintain the city walls. This was made when William of Wykeham, Bishop of Winchester, founded the college in 1379. New College is one of the largest colleges and is visited as much for its beautiful gardens, grounds and chapel as for the cloisters which feature in the film *Harry Potter and the Goblet of Fire*. A scene is set in the cloisters under the 200-year-old holm oak, where boy wizard Harry's nemesis, Draco Malfoy, is turned into a ferret.

7. **Binsey**. A village on the north-east side of Port Meadow on the outskirts of Oxford. In 1879, a line of poplars was cut down, leading to Hopkins writing his reflective poem 'Binsey Poplars'. This Jesuit poet (1844-1889) typically contemplates a theme from nature in his poetry and then extrapolates his observations into a wider theological motif. In fact, the poplars in questions grew back relatively quickly.

8. **Harcourt Arboretum at Nuneham Courtenay** was created by landscape architect William Gilpin for Archbishop Vernon Harcourt, who wanted an avenue with pines and redwood on the approach to his house. The Arboretum now covers 130 acres and is part of the Oxford Botanic Garden and Arboretum.

9. **Waterperry Gardens, near Wheatley.** Between 1932 and 1971, several generations of female gardeners were trained at Waterperry School of Horticulture under the watchful eye of its founder, Beatrix Havergal. Now the extensive ornamental gardens are open and include a cafe, a fascinating museum of agricultural implements, and a garden shop selling specimen plants and gifts.

10. Emperor Naruhito of Japan (r.2019–) spent 1983–85, which he says were the happiest days of his life, at Merton College researching the Upper Thames. You can read all about his experiences in the 2006 monograph *The Thames and I.*

8

Fun and Games

Mens sana in corpore sano, or a healthy mind in a healthy body. This is clearly sensible although perhaps these days young people, especially students, spend less time on the playing fields than in the past. Despite this, the standard of sport remains high.

1. Who set a world record in Oxford in June 1954?

2. What honour is awarded to University of Oxford students who take part in sports against Cambridge University?

3. Where is the annual Rugby Union match between Oxford and Cambridge universities played?

4. What is the name of the week in summer when rowing races take place on the River Thames?

5. Which disgraced newspaper magnate, publisher and politician previously owned Oxford United Football Club?

6. Which game, much loved by King Henry VIII, is still played in Oxford?

7. If you woke up in a punt, how would you tell if you were in Oxford or Cambridge?

8. What is the length of the annual Oxford and Cambridge Boat Race?

   a) 5 miles and 275 yards
   b) 3 miles and 473 yards
   c) 4 miles and 274 yards

9. Which impressive golfing feat was achieved within the confines of Christ Church?

10. What is Vincent's Club?

Chapter 8 Answers

1. **Roger Bannister** (1929-2018), a junior doctor at St Mary's Hospital in London, had studied medicine at Exeter College. He broke the four-minute-mile barrier on the Iffley Road athletic track on 4 June 1954. He was assisted by pacemakers Christopher Chataway and Christopher Brasher. Brasher later went on to set up the London Marathon in 1981. Bannister had a distinguished career as a neurologist and became Master of Pembroke College (1985-93). His various achievements are honoured by a memorial stone in London's Westminster Abbey alongside the burials of Isaac Newton, Charles Darwin and Stephen Hawking.

2. **A Blue.** A full Blue is awarded for mainstream sports such as rugby, tennis, hockey, cricket and squash. Half Blues are awarded for more niche sports such as real tennis and fencing. Cambridge University also awards Blues. The expression Blue refers to the team colours worn: Oxford's are navy blue and Cambridge's are duck egg blue.

3. **Twickenham, in West London.** The Varsity match has taken place at Rugby Union's most famous ground since 1927, although the fixture itself dates back to 1872. Rugby Football had been played at Rugby School in Warwickshire since the early 1820s, where the ball could be held or kicked; apparently it was when William Webb Ellis ran with the ball in his hand that the game became distinctly different from soccer.

4. **Eights Week**. Because the Thames is too narrow for boats to race side by side, races are linear with the college crews competing to catch up or 'bump' the boat ahead. Once bumped, boats drop out and, for the next race, the faster boat is promoted up the line. The leading boat at the end of the week of competition is declared Head of the River. College balls traditionally take place in Eights Week and, in the past, male undergraduates asked young women to accompany them to the May Balls at their colleges whilst also taking time to walk by the river and enjoy the rowing.

5. **Robert Maxwell** (1923–1991) drowned in the Mediterranean in mysterious circumstances near his motor yacht, *The Lady Ghislaine*. The club's stadium is now owned by, and named after, Firoz Kassam, a property developer who was previously club chairman.

6. **Real (aka Royal) Tennis.** A court on Merton Lane is used regularly by Oxford University students and others to play this game. The court layout mirrors a medieval courtyard with pitched roofs along three sides, netting, windows and other obstacles. Lawn tennis evolved from this game with similar scoring, net and rackets. There are around fifty courts worldwide including at Hampton Court Palace, Queen's Club, London and Lord's Cricket Ground.

7. **Punt design varies slightly between Oxford and Cambridge, as do punting methods.** In Oxford, you stand inside the punt at the stern, or back, with the flat platform at the front, or bow, ahead of you. In Cambridge, you stand on the platform. In both places, you move the punt by placing a long pole in the water and pushing it. Punts were originally used for moving goods around, and probably also for fishing.

8. **c) Around 4 miles and 274 yards**, or 6.8 kilometres, from Putney to Mortlake on the River Thames in London. The race first took place in 1829; by 1856 it was an annual event, though there were no races during the two world wars, nor one in 2020 at the beginning of the Covid-19 pandemic. In 2021, the race took place on the river Great Ouse near Cambridge but without specatators. With roughly eighty victories on each side, Cambridge have been ahead since 1930. There was one dead

heat in 1877. The race originally took place at Henley. Many rowers are now virtually professional oarsmen, attending the universities as graduate students.

9. In 1952, Peter Gardiner-Hill (b.1926), captain of the Oxford University golfing society and later captain of the Royal & Ancient, Scotland's most distinguished golfing society, chipped a golf ball from outside his rooms in Christ Church's Peckwater Quad into the pond in Tom Quad. Not only is it impossible to see the intended trajectory, but this involves pitching the ball around 40ft in the air and carrying it around 300ft across the top of two substantial buildings, before landing it in a pond which is about 12ft wide.

10. A club almost entirely made up of those who have won Oxford Blues. Named after the High Street stationers who, in 1863, provided this club with rooms where they first gathered.

9

Pillars of Wisdom

Oxford's reputation and success as a centre of academic excellence is underpinned by its outstanding libraries, museums and galleries. An arrangement was established by Sir Thomas Bodley with the Stationers' Company in London for his new library to receive copies of all books published; this makes the Bodleian a Copyright Library. Today, for example, it contains over 12 million books, receiving more than 1,000 new publications a day.

1. Match the museum or library to the subject:

    a) Bate
    b) Pitt Rivers
    c) Sackler
    d) Taylorian
    e) The Oxford Museum
    f) The Story Museum

    i) Ethnography
    ii) Local History
    iii) Modern Languages
    iv) Children's Literature & Storytelling
    v) Music
    vi) Classics (Latin and Greek) and Art History

2. Which museum doubled up as a nightclub in the detective series *Lewis*?

3. Which family helped finance the most recent expansion and redevelopment of the Bodleian Library?

4. Which Anglo-Saxon king is linked to one of the best known artefacts in the Ashmolean Museum?

5. Which educational institution started life in the basement of the Taylorian Library?

6. Whose early collection of rarities was once housed in what is now the History of Science Museum?

7. Which museum supervises an established colony of swifts?

8. Which museum in Oxford has recently embarked upon a major programme of decolonisation?

9. Where in Oxford did the famous debate take place on Charles Darwin's evolutionary theories?

10. Which library erected a memorial stone in 2018 to commemorate those who worked on Caribbean plantations?

Chapter 9 Answers

1. a) v; b) i; c) vi; d) iii; e) ii; f) iv.

2. The Sackler Library appears as The Portobello Nightclub in 'Music to Die For' in the 2008 second series of *Lewis*. This series was a sequel to the award-winning *Inspector Morse* detective series which ran from 1987 to 2000.

3. The £80 million extension and upgrade to the Bodleian Library was underwritten by a £25 million gift from the UK-based part of the **Weston family**, whose portfolio of interests includes Associated British Foods, Fortnum & Mason on London's Piccadilly and Primark.

4. **King Alfred of Wessex** (r.871–99). The Alfred Jewel is one of the most beautiful items in the Ashmolean. It is thought to be the top of an aestel or pointer which was used to follow a line of text in a medieval manuscript. It's inscribed with '*Aelfred mec heht gewyrcan*' (King Alfred ordered me to be made). In King Alfred's effort to promote literacy, he circulated Pope Gregory's tract, *Pastoral Care*, perhaps accompanied by an aestel.

5. Art classes initiated by John Henry Brookes, in the basement of the **Taylorian Institute**, led to the setting up of the Oxford Technical School, the foundation of Oxford Polytechnic, and a move to Headington in 1949. In 1992, it was renamed Oxford Brookes University which now educates

over 20,000 students, including 5,000 postgraduates. It offers a wide range of subjects including some which are more vocational, and has been ranked amongst the top fifty universities in the world.

6. **Elias Ashmole.** Oxford University provided this building in 1683 to house the collection that had been donated by this polymath and antiquarian, thus establishing the country's first public museum. Many of the objects had come into Ashmole's possession from the collection of a father and son duo, both called John Tradescant, who were gardeners and travellers. One of the best-known artefacts is a deerskin mantle decorated with cowrie shells that belonged

to Powhatan, a Native American chief. His daughter, Pocahontas, who married John Rolfe, one of the early colonists, is a famous historical figure who visited and died in England in 1616/17. The move to larger premises came in 1894, when the Ashmolean focused more on art and archaeology, leaving the original building to become the Museum of the History of Science by 1924.

7. Swifts have been nesting annually in the tower at the **Museum of Natural History** on South Parks Road and can be seen on webcams between April and August. The colony of European swifts, which migrate to and from Central Africa, has been monitored and researched since 1947, contributing significantly to the understanding of this bird which is struggling due to a decline in suitable nesting sites.

8. **Pitt Rivers Museum.** Located at the back of the Museum of Natural History, this is an archaeological and ethnographic collection of nearly 500,000 objects from all parts of the world. It grew from the 26,000-item collection given by General Pitt Rivers in 1884. Until recently the collection displayed shrunken heads from South America, which were used in rituals to possess the souls of dead people. These along with many other items have been removed from public display to respect the cultures and beliefs of people from whom these items were obtained in the past. The museum is engaged in many other initiatives to reimagine the collection in a more appropriate light

9. At the **Natural History Museum** on South Parks Road in June 1860. The debaters were the evolutionist Thomas Henry Huxley and the Bishop of Oxford, Samuel Wilberforce. During the

debate Wilberforce famously asked Huxley if he was descended from an ape on his maternal or his paternal side, to which he replied, 'I would rather be the offspring of two apes than be a man and afraid to accept the truth.' The building was designed by the Anglo-Irish architect Benjamin Woodward of the firm Deane and Woodward.

10. The Codrington Library, All Souls College. The Codrington family owned estates in the West Indies where the labour of enslaved people from Africa was routinely used. Christopher Codrington, who had been educated at Oxford, left £10,000 in 1710 to endow the library, completed by Nicholas Hawksmoor in 1751. Codrington also endowed Codrington College, Barbados, which now focuses on theology. All Souls College, which has no graduate or undergraduate students, and an endowment of at least £420m, put up a plaque in 2017 at the entrance to the library to commemorate those who had worked on Codrington family Carribbean plantations. It also set up a £150,000 scholarship scheme to fund graduate students from the Caribbean studying in Oxford and made a five year grant to Codrington College in Barbados. In late 2020 it was announced the library will no longer bear the Codrington name. The statue of Christopher Codrington in imperial attire remains in situ in the library, however, but is to have digital displays nearby to contextulise and explain it's provenance. In 2021, All Souls gave £1m to an Oxford programme to support black students; there is also to be an Annual lecture about the transatlantic slave trade and further support provided to Codrington College and to graduates from the Carribbean coming to Oxford.

10

When the Saints Go Marching In

Religion and the observation of saints' days was a major part of medieval life and early scholarship in Oxford revolved around Christian teaching. Saints featured significantly, as revering them might hasten your passage to heaven. They were also thought to have healing powers.

1. Who is the patron saint of Oxford?

   a) St Ebbe
   b) St Mary
   c) St Frideswide
   d) St Cecilia

2. Name the fair which takes place in Oxford in early September.

3. Which is the oldest surviving building in Oxford?

4. Which Oxford churchman was canonised by Pope Francis in 2019?

5. Which saint's day caused a riot?

6. Which Italianate church was built for the workers of the Oxford University Press?

7. Whose martyrdom is depicted in a stained-glass window in the St Lucy Chapel in Christ Church Cathedral?

8. Why can you see broad-rimmed hats trailing tassels on the stone carvings and metalwork around Christ Church?

9. Members of which ethnic minority were burnt in Oxford on St Brice's Day, 1002?

   a) Danes
   b) Jews
   c) Celts
   d) Normans

10. Which saints are on the facade of Lincoln College?

   a) St Mary and St Mildred
   b) St Bernard and St Mary
   c) St John and St Hugh
   d) St James and St Hugh

Chapter 10 Answers

1. c) St Frideswide. This medieval princess refused to marry Prince Algar of Mercia, so she fled from Oxford and hid nearby at Binsey. Her suitor continued to pursue her, but legend says he was struck blind by a thunderbolt, leaving Frideswide free to found a nunnery and perform various healing miracles. She eventually returned to Oxford and founded a religious order. Subsequently, this became an Augustinian priory, the site of which was used by Thomas Wolsey in 1524 for building Cardinal College, which later became Christ Church.

2. St Giles' Fair takes place on the wide thoroughfare of St Giles on the first Monday and Tuesday following the first Sunday after St Giles' Day, which is 1 September. Originally a parish gathering or wake, by the late eighteenth century it had become a showplace for unusual spectacles, human or otherwise. It is now a large funfair which is blessed by the Bishop of Oxford.

3. St Michael at the North Gate (although St George's Tower at Oxford Castle also claims to be roughly the same age). The Saxon ragstone tower, built in 1040, is all that is left of the gatehouse which marked the western entrance to Oxford. It became the Bocardo Prison, where Thomas Cranmer was imprisoned during the reign of Queen Mary Tudor, who was nicknamed Bloody Mary. Cranmer watched his colleagues,

Bishops Latimer and Ridley, being burnt alive on nearby Broad Street in 1555, having refused to recant their Protestant beliefs. Cranmer followed them to the stake in 1556.

4. St John Henry Newman (1801–1890). This nineteenth-century theologian and poet was one of the founders of the Oxford Tractarian movement which promoted the return to greater ritual in the liturgy. Newman studied at Trinity College and was a Fellow at Oriel. He preached regular sermons or tracts at the University Church of St Mary the Virgin, where he was vicar. By 1845, however, Newman converted to Roman Catholicism, was ordained and became a cardinal. He was beatified in 2010 following several associated miracles and was declared a saint in 2019.

5. St Scholastica. A serious riot broke out between the students and the townsfolk at the Swindlestock Tavern on 10 February 1355, lasting for several days and leading to many deaths on both sides. St Scholastica was the sister of St Benedict of Nursia, who established the Rule of St Benedict for monastic communities. The City of Oxford was making amends for the riot until the middle of the nineteenth century.

6. St Barnabas Church in Jericho is the work of the Victorian architect Arthur Blomfield and was built in 1872. Its campanile (or bell tower) is particularly distinctive. The Oxford University Press moved to west Oxford in 1828. The church also served the people working at the nearby Eagle Ironworks.

7. **St Thomas à Becket**, Chancellor to Henry II and then Archbishop of Canterbury. An argument led to Thomas's violent death in Canterbury Cathedral in 1170. By 1172, he had been canonised as a Christian martyr, becoming one of the most popular medieval saints. This window depicting St Thomas includes some of the country's oldest remaining stained glass, and was popular with pilgrims who visited the cathedral. During the sixteenth century, St Thomas's face was removed from the window because the adoration of saints was discouraged by Protestant reformers. It has since been replaced by a blank piece of glass.

8. Christ Church was originally founded by Cardinal Thomas Wolsey in 1524 as Cardinal College. The hats refer to the red broad-brimmed papal cardinal's hat which Wolsey would have worn. On Wolsey's fall from grace in 1529/30, following his failure to secure a divorce for Henry VIII from his Spanish wife, Catherine of Aragon, his property, including this partially built college, was seized by the king. After an initial false start, Henry VIII eventually re-founded the college as Christ Church in 1546.

9. a) Danes. For many years marauding Danes attacked eastern England from their native Scandinavia. In the late ninth century, King Alfred made a deal with the Danes which gave the Danes land to the north and east and protected the land of Wessex to the west. By the early eleventh century, the raids increased again. King Aethelred married Emma of Normandy and appealed to the Normans to stop sheltering the Vikings. He also ordered the massacre of all settled Danes on Saxon soil. The Danes in Oxford sought sanctuary in St Frideswide's chapel but it was set alight with significant loss of life.

10. a) St Mary and St Mildred. These 2009 statues by Stephen Cox can be seen above the entrance gate. Lincoln College was founded in 1427. St Mildred was a seventh-century Anglo-Saxon princess who became a nun rather than marry. She is associated with church security as she is depicted with geese around her feet; many churches kept geese to raise the alarm against intruders.

11

Eat, Drink
and be Merry!

We're now halfway through our exploration of the City of Oxford, its history and customs, past and present, and are surely in need of a break! Where better than in one of the many hostelries around the town. Taking care of your brain is one thing but that's all very well if your more physical needs are not met. It's not a coincidence that one of the most fractious confrontations between the town and university students took place in the Swindlestock Tavern in 1355 following an argument about poor quality wine. This lasted for three days and left nearly seventy students and unrecorded numbers of townsfolk dead (the record of the event was kept by the university). Fortunately, standards have risen since then and the City of Oxford has many excellent pubs, cafes and restaurants catering to every taste and budget.

1. Where in Oxford would you be ill-advised to wear a tie?

2. Where can you buy ingredients for an Oxford-themed cheese and sausage sandwich?

3. Which riverside pub was a favourite of fictional detective Inspector Morse?

4. Which Michelin-starred hotel and restaurant is to be found just outside Oxford?

5. Where was the first coffee shop in England?

6. Which pub was near the home of a Pre-Raphaelite muse?

7. Which Oxford hotel has a bar named after a fictional detective?

8. Who first marketed a preserved fruit spread?

9. Which Commonwealth Prime Minister set a record for drinking a yard of ale?

10. Which fish do we have to thank for the creation of the Bodleian Library?

Chapter 11 Answers

1. **The Bear on Alfred Street**. Since the 1950s, the landlord has built up a collection of neckwear by cutting off the bottom of ties which catch his eye in exchange for half a pint of beer. There's been a pub here since the thirteenth century, although this building dates from the sixteenth century. The name refers to bear-baiting, which was a popular activity, so live bears may also have been kept nearby.

2. **The Covered Market**. This centrally located market was established in 1774 to take traders off the surrounding streets. In it you can find specialist shops selling food and other items. The Oxford Sausage, available here, will include veal as well as pork in a traditional sausage recipe. Oxford Blue Cheese, a stilton-type cheese, was launched to great success in 1995 by the Oxford Cheese Company which also operates from the Covered Market.

3. **The Trout Inn at Wolvercote**. Morse also frequented The Perch at Binsey and the White Horse in Broad Street, which is the smallest pub in the town. Morse, like his creator Colin Dexter, a long-time resident of Oxford, was keen on real ale. Morse claims he can only really think properly with a pint in his hand. His sidekick, Sergeant Lewis, always has to foot the bill, however, as Morse is always short of money. The Trout is also the childhood home of Malcolm Polstead, the

11-year-old protagonist in *La Belle Sauvage*, the prequel to Philip Pullman's *His Dark Materials* trilogy.

4. **Le Manoir aux Quat'Saisons at Great Milton.** Self-taught chef Raymond Blanc opened a small restaurant in Summertown in Oxford in 1977, which won Egon Ronay Restaurant of the Year and a Michelin star. This success allowed him to buy a fifteenth century manor house in 1984, which he built up to be an award-winning hotel and a two Michelin-starred restaurant. It's now part of the Belmond Hotel Group.

5. **Oxford High Street.** During the Protectorate (1649–1660), Jews were encouraged to return to England having been expelled in 1290 by King Edward I. One, named Jacob, opened a coffee house at Angel Inn, selling a new Turkish drink; another followed nearby which still stands as Queen's Lane Coffee House. The Angel Inn no longer exists, although The Grand Cafe stands on the site. Coffee houses became popular meeting places. In London they evolved into financial institutions such as Lloyd's insurance market and the Stock Exchange.

6. **The Turf Tavern.** Jane Burden lived on St Helen's Passage, running from New College Lane to Holywell Street past the Turf Tavern. This pub incorporates part of the medieval city wall. Exeter student and Pre-Raphaelite artist William Morris was struck by her beauty and married her in 1859, despite the differences in their backgrounds. She was also muse to Dante Gabriel Rossetti, with whom she became romantically involved. Her distinctive looks feature in many paintings by this group of artists.

7. **The Randolph Hotel by Graduate Hotels.** The Morse Bar is named after Colin Dexter's fictional detective, Inspector Morse. Several episodes included the hotel in the action. This mid-Victorian Gothic revival building is named after an eighteenth-century university benefactor, Francis Randolph.

8. **Frank Cooper**, although it was his wife, Sarah Jane Cooper's marmalade recipe which got the venture off the ground in 1874. Cooper's Oxford Orange Marmalade, in its various thicknesses, is the staple of many British breakfasts, even going on Captain Scott's doomed 1912 expedition to the South Pole. It was originally sold in a High Street shop but later manufactured in the Jam Factory on Park End Street.

9. Australian politician and Rhodes Scholar **Bob Hawke** (1929-2019) downed 1.7 litres or a yard of ale in eleven seconds in the mid-1950s. There is debate as to whether this took place in the dining hall of University College or at the Turf Tavern, suggesting the feat may have taken place more than once. Hawke claimed this stunt did much to improve his political ratings: he was Australian Prime Minister from 1983-91.

10. Pilchards. In early 1602, Sir Thomas Bodley (1545-1613) was able to finance the establishment of the library (which takes his name) because his wife, Ann, had been previously married to a wealthy Totnes fish merchant and town mayor, who made his fortune from selling pilchards. The Bodleian is a copyright library, due to an arrangement Bodley made with the Stationers' Company in London and now has over 12 million books, many of which have to be kept in underground storage or stacks, some now located 30 miles away in Swindon.

12

Who's Who?

Over the years the University of Oxford has tended to attract many of the brightest and the best of each generation. In certain fields, politics in particular, Oxford has produced more than its fair share of high-profile figures both at home and abroad. Graduates from this university have also been awarded over fifty Nobel Prizes. I include here a modest selection of distinguished men and women who have been students at Oxford University or are otherwise associated with the City of Oxford.

1. Name the US President awarded a Rhodes Scholarship to study at Oxford University:

    a) J.F. Kennedy
    b) Barack Obama
    c) William Clinton
    d) F.D. Roosevelt

2. Who's the odd one out and did *not* study at Oxford University?

    a) King Abdullah II of Jordan
    b) Norman Manley
    c) Mahatma Gandhi
    d) Bob Hawke
    e) King Harald V of Norway
    f) Price Leopold of Saxe Coburg Gotha

3. How many British Prime Ministers have been educated a) at Oxford University, and b) at Christ Church?

4. Name the Oxford student who is credited with inventing the World Wide Web:

   a) Stephen Hawking
   b) Tim Berners-Lee
   c) Alan Turing
   d) Howard Florey

5. Name five female Oxford University graduates who went on to lead their countries.

6. Who never grew up?

7. Who was the first black African to be awarded a degree by Oxford University?

8. Which twentieth-century Arabist was brought up in Polstead Road, Oxford?

9. Which churchman founded a now worldwide organisation to support those despairing and at risk of suicide?

10. Which Oxford University graduate was part of an unsuccessful plot to assassinate Adolf Hitler?

Chapter 12 Answers

1. c) **William Clinton.** Clinton won a Rhodes Scholarship in 1968 and was given accommodation by University College just off Magpie Lane. Cecil Rhodes (1853-1902) made a fortune mining diamonds in South Africa and Zimbabwe (previously Rhodesia). His legacy now funds 100 normally two-year scholarships to study at Oxford for those from a selection of countries, many of which had historic links to the British Empire. A statue of Cecil Rhodes on the High Street facade of Oriel College is controversial, as many of Rhodes's views are considered by many to be racist and imperialist, leading to a campaign to remove the statue with the slogan, 'Rhodes must Fall'. More recently, scholars have come from a wider range of countries and the Trust operates on a very different range of values and objectives. Since 1929, the scheme has been administered from Rhodes House (presently undergoing a £37m refurbishment) on South Parks Road. One Rhodes Scholar, James Fulbright, went on to found a scholarship programme of his own.

2. c) **Mahatma Gandhi.** All of the others studied at Oxford University. Gandhi (1869-1948) was born in India, studied law at the Inner Temple in London, and then worked in South Africa. His various experiences there, including of racial segregation, led him subsequently to become engaged in Indian politics. He adopted a policy of peaceful protest and ascetic living and was assassinated in 1948. To show how

his values are admired in this country, there is a statue of him in London's Parliament Square and a roof boss in the Church of St Mary the Virgin, Oxford.

3. As of the time of writing, twenty-eight British Prime Ministers have been educated at Oxford University, with thirteen of them having studied at Christ Church. The debating style of the Houses of Parliament favours experienced public speakers, so many politicians learnt their trade at the Oxford Union Society, which supports and encourages debating skills. Oxford also teaches PPE (Politics, Philosophy & Economics) which attracts students with political aspirations. The majority of Prime Ministers in the last fifty years have been Oxford educated: Boris Johnson, Theresa May, David Cameron, Tony Blair, Margaret Thatcher, Edward Heath and Harold Wilson all studied at Oxford University.

4. b) Tim Berners-Lee (b.1955). A student at The Queen's College in the 1970s, where he studied physics, Berners-Lee promoted the sharing of data whilst working at Cern Laboratories in Geneva. He did not patent or make a charge for access to the system he established, which has transformed the way information is shared and accessed across the world. He has received many honours for his work in this area.

5. Benazir Bhutto (1953-2007), Pakistan; Margaret Thatcher (1925-2013), United Kingdom; Indira Gandhi (1917-1984), India; Aung San Suu Kyi (b. 1945), Myanmar. Theresa May, (b. 1956), United Kingdom.

6. **Michael Llewelyn Davies** was one of the five sons of Arthur and Sylvia Llewelyn Davies who were befriended as children by author James Barrie, who met them in London's Kensington Gardens. Barrie took his inspiration for **Peter Pan** from the characters of the Llewelyn Davies boys, and wrote a stage play which was performed in 1904 and later adapted by Barrie into a book, published as *Peter and Wendy* in 1911. Michael tragically drowned in 1921 whilst swimming with a friend in the Thames near Oxford. He had been studying at Christ Church, and his memorial is in the cloister.

7. **Christian Cole**, who was born in Sierra Leone, studied Classics at University College, Oxford, initially as a non-collegiate student and then from 1877 as a member of University College. He is commemorated on a plaque in Logic Lane. He went on to study for the bar and became the first black African to be a member of the Inner Temple.

8. **T.E. Lawrence**, otherwise known as Lawrence of Arabia, lived with his family at 2 Polstead Road, Oxford, between 1896 and 1921. He was a key participant in the politics of the Middle East during and after World War One. His account of his work in Arabia, *The Seven Pillars of Wisdom*, was published to great acclaim in 1927. He became a Fellow of All Souls College in 1920 and was killed in a motorcycle accident in Dorset in 1935.

9. **The Samaritans** were founded in 1953 by Anglican vicar Chad Varah, who had studied at Keble College in the early 1930s. The voluntary listening and befriending service has saved countless lives by providing a voice and support for those in crisis.

10. Adam von Trott. He studied briefly at Mansfield in 1927 and again as a Rhodes Scholar in 1931–33 at Balliol. He visited England during the later 1930s to warn against appeasement. He joined the Nazi Party to be able to get close to his nemesis, but was arrested after the failed 1944 bomb plot to kill Adolf Hitler and was executed later that year. His name is included in a memorial plaque in Balliol College for students killed in World War Two.

13

The Crown

Although Oxford has moved in and out of royal favour over the years, in the seventeenth-century civil war it was particularly prominent. In 1644, King Charles I moved his capital to Oxford because London, the home of Parliament, was proving too challenging. Papers recovered after World War Two showed Oxford avoided being bombed because Adolf Hitler selected it to be his administrative headquarters if he had been victorious.

1. Which king's brother donated his books to the university?

2. Which prince befriended Alice Liddell whilst a student at Christ Church?

3. Which English monarch was refused permission to borrow a book from the Bodleian Library?

4. Which monarch is seen giving a book to an allegorical figure of Learning, representing the University of Oxford?

    a) King James II
    b) King James I
    c) King Charles II
    d) Queen Elizabeth I

5. Name two former royal palaces in or near Oxford

6. Who escaped from Oxford Castle during a siege?

7. Where did the future Edward VIII, when Prince of Wales,
   study when he was a student at Oxford in 1912?

8. What's significant about a mulberry tree in Balliol
   College?

9. What building near Oxford impressed George III?

10. Where, near Oxford, did Henry VIII bring Catherine of
    Aragon for health reasons?

Chapter 13 Answers

1. Humfrey, Duke of Gloucester, younger brother of King Henry V, donated over 280 books and manuscripts to the university in the decade before his death in 1447. The university had previously possessed very few books as teaching was conducted orally. Although many of these donated books and manuscripts were destroyed during the reign of Edward VI in 1550 as being too Roman Catholic, the space built to house his collection remains one of the finest reading rooms within the Bodleian Library. Henry V himself (1386–1422) is said to have studied at The Queen's College.

2. Prince Leopold, youngest son of Queen Victoria and Prince Albert, became close to Alice Liddell, the daughter of the Dean of Christ Church, whilst studying there in 1872. Prince Leopold married Princess Helena of Waldeck but named his daughter Alice. Prince Leopold was a pallbearer at the funeral in 1876 of Alice's sister Edith. He died of complications surrounding his haemophilia in 1884. Alice Liddell married another student from Christ Church, Reginald Hargreaves, and named one of her sons Leopold (sadly killed in World War One). Alice was the model for the *Alice in Wonderland* stories written for her and her siblings by Charles Dodgson, aka Lewis Carroll, who taught mathematics at Christ Church. She lived until 1934.

3. **King Charles I.** By 1644, Charles I had set up court in Oxford, a Royalist city. He lodged at Christ Church and his wife Henrietta Maria, a French Catholic and the focus of much of the anti-Catholic feeling, lodged at nearby Merton College. Archbishop William Laud, a High Anglican, was Chancellor of the University in 1636 when the Canterbury Quad at his old college, St John's, was completed, incorporating statues of the King and Queen by Hubert Le Sueur.

4. **b) King James I.** A 1620 statue of the king surmounts the Tower of the Five Orders in the central quadrangle of the Bodleian Library. The tower includes pillars of Tuscan, Doric, Ionic, Corinthian and Composite styles. King James I was an educated man who said that, had he not been king,

he would have opted to be a 'university man'. He is shown giving a copy of his theological writings to a female figure representing Learning, clearly representing the University of Oxford, with a fanfare being played alongside by Fame. This seems a bit ironic as women were not awarded degrees at the University of Oxford for another 300 years.

5. **Beaumont Palace and Woodstock Palace**. Beaumont Palace was the birthplace of two royal princes and sons of King Henry II: Richard I (r.1189–99), nicknamed The Lionheart due to his crusading exploits, and King John of Magna Carta fame (r.1199–1216). This palace was situated in the centre of modern Oxford on Beaumont Street near the Ashmolean Museum. Woodstock Palace, 10 miles north west of Oxford, was still in use in the sixteenth century when it was used to imprison Princess Elizabeth, and its parkland was enclosed with thick walls to keep Henry I's menagerie of lions and leopards secure. Henry I's grandson, Henry II, enjoyed visiting his mistress, Rosamund Clifford, there. She was buried just outside the City of Oxford at Godstow Nunnery, which has not survived.

6. **Empress Matilda**, disguised in a white nightgown, escaped over the snow to Abingdon in 1142, whilst Oxford was besieged by her cousin Stephen of Blois. This was during a civil war known as The Anarchy, when chroniclers said that 'God and his angels slept.' Matilda was the only surviving legitimate child of Henry I, following the death of her brother Prince William in the wreck of the *White Ship*, which lead to Stephen and others contesting her right to the throne. Although Stephen was victorious, being crowned king in 1135, it was Matilda's son Henry who succeeded him in 1154.

7. **Magdalen College**. He had rooms in the fifteenth-century tower and travelled around the town in a Daimler. David, as he was known by his family before he became king in 1936, was a charming, popular and handsome Prince of Wales. His reign was short, however, as he abdicated in December 1936 so he could marry twice-divorced Mrs Wallis Simpson. His brother, Bertie, succeeded to the throne as George VI. He is the father of Queen Elizabeth II (b.1926), who has reigned since his death in 1952.

8. **The mulberry tree at Balliol College is said to be over 400 years old**. There is some dispute as to whether it was planted by Elizabeth I or by Charles II. A long time ago, either way.

9. **Blenheim Palace**. This stately home near the site of the royal palace at Woodstock was built with £240,000 given to John Churchill as thanks from a grateful nation for his victory at the Battle of Blenheim in 1704 against King Louis XIV of France. When George III visited he remarked, 'We do not have anything as fine as this.' Blenheim is the only secular non-royal building known as a palace. Elevated to the Dukedom of Marlborough, his descendant Winston Churchill, who led the country in World War Two, was born at Blenheim in 1874 as his grandfather was the 7th Duke of Marlborough.

10. **St Margaret's Well at Binsey** was a *triacle*, or healing well, frequented by St Frideswide in the eighth century. Henry VIII brought Catherine here hoping it would enhance her fertility. She had given birth to one daughter who had survived (Mary Tudor), but no male had survived. The *Alice in Wonderland* stories include a 'treacle well', wordplay on the word *triacle*.

14

Heavens Above

Religion, both in theory and in practice, has been the backbone of the University of Oxford since its inception. Oxford was a place for scholars and debaters and was the focal point for religious debate and dissension, with new religious ideas frequently emerging here. Oxford also had more than its fair share of deaths associated with religious beliefs. There is a memorial in the University Church of St Mary the Virgin to the twenty-three people who died for their beliefs between 1539 and 1681. On a brighter note, the existence of a well-established and influential medieval Jewish community in Oxford has led to the Bodleian Library having a world-class collection of Hebrew manuscripts.

1. Where in Oxford were three men burnt for their Protestant belief?

2. Which eighteenth-century Oxford graduate founded a non-conformist Christian sect?

3. Match the Permanent Private Halls to their affiliated religions:

a) Regent's Park College

b) St Benet's Hall

c) Blackfriars

d) Wycliffe Hall

e) St Stephen's House

f) Campion Hall

i) Roman Catholic (Benedictine)

ii) Evangelical

iii) Church of England/ High Anglican

iv) Baptist

v) Roman Catholic (Jesuit)

vi) Roman Catholic (Dominican)

4. Why is the path running along the back of Merton College called Dead Man's Walk?

5. Which college chapel is unique in having access directly onto the public street?

6. Which fourteenth-century religious movement promoted the vernacular and advocated the return of the established Church to poverty?

7. Which Oxford church porch was cited in a treason trial?

8. Where is Oxford's synagogue?

9. Where is there a centre for Islamic Studies in Oxford?

10. Where in Oxford were four Roman Catholics hanged in 1589?

Chapter 14 Answers

1. **On Broad Street**, opposite the entrance to Balliol College, marked by a cross on the road. In 1555, Bishops Hugh Latimer and Nicholas Ridley were burnt for refusing to renounce their Protestant faith. They were followed in 1556 by Archbishop Thomas Cranmer. They had been core promoters of Protestantism under the reign of King Edward VI (r.1547–53), but when he died, his sister Mary (r.1553–58) was determined to re-establish the Roman Catholic faith. The Martyrs' Memorial was erected in 1843 on nearby St Giles as a warning to those who supported the Anglo-Catholic movement, which promoted the return of the Church of England to more ritualistic practices as seen in Roman Catholic liturgy. The memorial is modelled on thirteenth-century Eleanor Crosses, a replica of which can be seen outside London's Charing Cross station.

2. **John Wesley**, a student at Christ Church and a fellow at Lincoln College, founded Methodism. This was initially a purely religious movement, relying on faith alone and which promoted living by a particular routine or method. It came to have a political focus and was especially attractive in the industrial cities of the Midlands and the North, as well as the mining communities in Wales. John Wesley was a regular preacher at the University Church of St Mary the Virgin in Radcliffe Square. His brother Charles Wesley was a prolific hymn writer.

3. Private halls all have religious affiliations and so have not sought collegiate status in order to retain their independence. Many colleges started life as private halls but then applied for collegiate status. a) iv; b) i; c) vi; d) ii; e) iii; f) v.

4. This path follows the route, outside the medieval city walls, originally taken by the Jewish community, accompanying their dead to their burial ground on the present day site of Magdalen College, which was founded in 1458. The burial ground was then moved a few hundred yards south but was again repossessed in 1621 to create the Botanic Gardens. There is a memorial by the Botanic Gardens to commemorate both of these Jewish graveyards. Oxford had one of the larger medieval Jewish communities, which is especially well documented due to its links to the university.

5. **Merton College Chapel** is accessible both from Merton Lane and from inside the college. The land for Merton College was acquired from Jacob, son of Moses of London, a Jewish merchant and local resident. There was already a parish church here, which became the college chapel on the understanding that local people as well as members of the college could access it. Merton was the first college to achieve self-governing collegiate status in 1264, although both Balliol College and University College challenge this.

6. **Lollardy, which was promulgated by John Wyclif.** The movement was strongly linked to St Edmund Hall, Oxford, whose principal, William Taylor, was burnt alive for his beliefs in 1423 at Smithfield in London. It advocated that the Bible and other religious texts should be available in English.

7. **The baroque porch on the south side of the University Church**, which was installed in 1637 during the chancellorship of Archbishop William Laud, caused great offence because of its baroque Anglo-Catholic iconography, including twisted pillars and a statue of the Virgin Mary. In 1640 Laud was put on trial for treason, but not executed until 1645, during the English Civil War.

8. **Richmond Road.** The existing 1974 building is shared by all Jewish sects in Oxford. It replaces an 1893 synagogue built by John Jacob Gardner. In medieval times, there was a synagogue on St Aldates, previously known as Great Jewry Street. The Jewish community in Oxford lived and worked close to the castle as their protection came from the Crown. It was King Edward I, however, who expelled the Jewish community from Oxford in 1290.

9. Marston Road. The Oxford Centre for Islamic Studies has existed since 1985 on various sites, but in 2017 moved to this permanent home. It is affiliated with the University of Oxford and promotes the multidisciplinary study of historic and contemporary Islamic culture and civilisation. Oxford is a multicultural city with a well-established Muslim community who worship at various sites around the city, the largest mosque being on Manzil Way in East Oxford.

10. On Longwall Street at the junction with Holywell Street. George Nichols, Richard Yaxley, Thomas Belson and Humphrey Pritchard were hung and then quartered, with their heads displayed at Oxford Castle. Although Oxford's Protestant martyrs are very well known, more Roman Catholics met their death for their belief during the sixteenth century in Oxford than Protestants.

15

Rocket Science

From its earlier roots as a centre of academic excellence, Oxford has been active in scientific investigation. The Royal Society emerged from meetings in Oxford in the 1650s and the university has educated many world-class scientists over the years, many of whom have won Nobel Prizes. Although, in the earlier twentieth century, Cambridge was more closely associated with scientific breakthroughs, Oxford University is now holding its own, having recently been given £150 million for a faculty dealing with artificial intelligence and associated ethical issues. Oxford Scientists such as Professors Sarah Gilbert and Andrew Pollard rose to prominence during the Covid-19 pandemic leading teams developing the pioneering Astra Zenica vaccine to provide protection against the virus. Oxford University's Regius Professor of Medicine John Hall sat on the UK vaccine task force.

1. Which Oxford-born physicist's ashes were interred at Westminster Abbey in 2018?

2. Which life-saving drug was developed commercially in Oxford in the 1940s?

3. Where in Oxford can you see a blackboard used by Albert Einstein?

4. Name the eighteenth-century society physician who left a legacy to Oxford University?

5. Which royalist physician's experimental work led to a reduction in bloodletting as a standard medical practice?

6. Which female scientist won a Nobel Prize in Chemistry in 1964?

7. Who had an observatory on New College Lane?

8. Which basic law of chemistry is commemorated by a plaque on Oxford's High Street?

9. Which early medieval scientist and thinker lived on Folly Bridge?

10. Which Oxford scientist proposed sending canaries down mines?

Chapter 15 Answers

1. Professor Stephen Hawking, who read Physics at University College, Oxford, before doing his postgraduate and professorial work in Cambridge, has been responsible for stimulating interest in physics and related subjects particularly among non-specialist audiences. Hawking was diagnosed in his early twenties with motor neurone disease. He communicated using computerised voice synthesis. His ashes are interred at Westminster Abbey, a rare honour these days and arranged at the invitation of the dean.

2. Penicillin. Even though Alexander Fleming made the initial discovery of penicillin at St Mary's Hospital in Paddington in 1928, it was Australian Howard Florey and his team, including Ernst Chain and Norman Heatley, who made the necessary progress and undertook clinical trials at the Radcliffe Infirmary. These enabled this drug to be produced commercially. Florey, Chain and Fleming were jointly awarded the Nobel Prize for their work in 1945.

3. The History of Science Museum. In 1931, the blackboard which Albert Einstein had written on during a lecture about his Theory of Relativity was preserved, indicating the early recognition of his groundbreaking work. Einstein visited Oxford regularly during the 1930s. There is an image of Einstein in a 1985 stained-glass window designed by Patrick Reyntiens in the dining hall at Christ Church.

4. **Dr John Radcliffe** (1650–1714). Physician to monarchs William and Mary, and also to Queen Anne, Radcliffe left £40,000 to Oxford University for a library. This circular building, originally conceived by Sir Nicholas Hawksmoor, but executed by James Gibbs in 1749 as a free-standing library, is now part of the Bodleian Library. Although a practical and popular doctor, Radcliffe was not known in his lifetime as a scholar, so his endowment raised a few eyebrows. Oxford also now has an observatory, a hospital and a science quarter named after Radcliffe.

5. **William Harvey** (1578–1657). His experimental work established that the heart was the muscle which pumped blood around the body. Harvey was educated at Cambridge but was physician to James I and came to Oxford with Charles I during the Civil War. He dedicated his seminal 1628 work on the circulation of the blood to Charles I. Harvey was Warden of Merton College between 1645 and 1646.

6. **Dorothy Crowfoot Hodgkin** (1910–1994) used X-ray crystallography to identify the three-dimensional features of molecules, including penicillin, vitamin B12 and insulin. She read chemistry at Somerville College and conducted her initial research in Cambridge before returning to Somerville in 1934. One of her students was Margaret Thatcher (*née* Roberts) who later became British Prime Minister (1978–90). Although they did not agree politically (Hodgkin was a life-long socialist), Thatcher is said to have regularly consulted her on scientific matters. Hodgkin is the first, and so far only, British woman to win this prize; the local paper chose the headline, 'Oxford Housewife wins Nobel Prize'.

7. **Edmond Halley** (1656–1742) was a student of The Queen's College and an early member of the Royal Society. He was Savilian Professor of Geometry and then Astronomer Royal. In 1705, he predicted the orbit of the comet which takes his name, last seen by the naked eye in 1986. It will return in 2061. Halley worked closely with Newton, Wren and Hooke, and financed the printing of the *Principia Mathematica* on which much of Newton's reputation is based.

8. Boyle's Law. Robert Boyle (1627–1691) observed that the volume of a gas varies inversely to the pressure it is under. Boyle, who was the son of the Earl of Lismore, worked closely with Robert Hooke (1635–1703), a talented scientist, albeit from a less privileged background. Hooke established the law of elasticity and was the first person to observe cells under a microscope. He was also involved in the creation of the Royal Society in London in 1660.

9. Roger Bacon (*c.*1214–1292). This charismatic philosopher, linguist, scientist, mathematician and Franciscan friar believed that studying these subjects would improve his theological understanding. Astronomy and cosmology were also fascinating to him. He had an observatory on Folly Bridge on the River Thames and was known during his life as Doctor Mirabilis. He is a good example of the type of scholar living in thirteenth-century Oxford: exploring and investigating the world around him and acting as a magnet to others.

10. John Scott Haldane (1860–1936) worked to improve workers' conditions and protect them from industrial diseases. Many of his experiments were conducted in a laboratory at his house in Linton Road, which later became the site of Wolfson College. Canaries were quicker to respond to the build-up of toxic gases, so their collapse would alert miners in adequate time to get safely above ground.

16

Bedtime Stories

Storytelling is part of our cultural make-up, and even more influential is telling stories to children. For those who have been lucky to have experienced the intimacy of bedtime storytelling, either as the deliverer or the recipient, it's clear that it provides lasting memories and comfort as well as stimulating the imagination. Oxford is a place of dreams and imaginings, with a lot of history thrown in, so it's not surprising that it has regularly stimulated the creative minds of students and academics alike. This has led to the production of a body of children's literature, particularly about fantasy worlds that have become entwined with our own. Mad Hatters, boastful toads, Hobbits, magic wardrobes and daemons are now familiar the world over, and they were mostly first imagined here.

1. To whose children did Charles Dodgson (aka Lewis Carroll) tell the stories which were published as *Alice in Wonderland* and *Alice Through the Looking Glass*?

2. Which films of a popular series of children's stories have used many key Oxford locations, either actual or recreated?

3. Where would you find an extensive range of children's books for sale in Oxford?

4. Who liked messing about in boats?

5. What was the previous use of the building which now houses Oxford's Story Museum?

6. Where is Alice's Shop?

7. Where is Will and Lyra's bench?

8. Where can you find a line-up of fictional characters commissioned by the Oxford Preservation Trust?

9. Which American student at Lincoln College created Thing One and Thing Two?

10. Which Edwardian author, best known for his tales of daring-do, won the Newdigate Prize for Poetry in 1898 and was elected President of the Oxford Union?

Chapter 16 Answers

1. **The children of the Dean of Christ Church**, Henry Liddell, one of whom was named Alice. On 4 July 1862, Charles Dodgson, mathematics tutor at Christ Church, took the Dean's children for a day out on the river. During this trip he told stories of the adventures of a child called Alice. The children asked him to write them down and they were published in 1865, under the pen name Lewis Carroll, with illustrations by the *Punch* artist, Tenniel. The firedogs in Christ Church dining hall with elongated necks may have inspired the extending necks which feature in the stories. In the dining hall, there is a 1985 stained-glass window by Patrick Reyntiens of both Dodgson and Alice. On or near 6 July, The Story Museum organises Alice's Day, a day of commemoration and fun around the city.

2. **The *Harry Potter* films**, based on the books by J.K. Rowling (b.1965). Christ Church Hall was recreated to be the dining hall at Hogwarts School of Witchcraft and Wizardry; New College, the Divinity School and Duke Humfrey's Library have also been regularly used for filming. The *Harry Potter* franchise, now worth over $25 billion worldwide, brings many visitors, young and old, to Oxford.

3. **Blackwell's Bookshop on Broad Street** has a fine collection of books of all sorts, including an excellent children's book department. It also has a subterranean room with 3 miles of bookshelves, which was, for a long time, the largest such room in the world. Blackwell's has been selling books in Oxford since 1879, and now has over forty shops, mostly in university towns. The publishing arm is no longer part of this group.

4. **Ratty from Kenneth Grahame's** *The Wind in the Willows*. Although his day job was working for the Bank of England, Kenneth Grahame must have remembered his school days at St Edward's School, Oxford, when he wrote this children's classic, evoking Edwardian England and creating the characters of Ratty, Mole, Toad and Badger. Published in 1908, Grahame bequeathed his royalties to the Bodleian Library. He is buried in Holywell Cemetery by St Cross Church.

5. **The most recent activity on this Pembroke Street site of Oxford's newest museum was a Post Office sorting office and the first automated telephone exchange in Oxford.** It has recently undergone an extensive redevelopment to provide a storytelling adventure for visitors young and old. In the twelfth century, a property on this site was owned by Jacob the Jew, son of Moses the Magnificent, and was used to house Hebrew scholars. These premises were taken over by Walter de Merton, who accommodated students there whilst his newly endowed college, which had been set up on Merton Street in 1264, was being developed.

6. Just opposite the entrance to Christ Church Meadow on St Aldates is a small red-fronted shop. This is where Charles Dodgson, aka Lewis Carroll, brought the Liddell children, including 9-year-old Alice, to buy sweets before exploring the riverbank and telling stories. It is called the sheep shop in *Alice Through the Looking Glass*, as the old lady who served Alice and her siblings had a voice like a bleating sheep.

7. **In Oxford's Botanic Gardens.** The chief protagonists in Philip Pullman's *His Dark Materials* fantasy novels, Will and Lyra, who occupy parallel worlds both of which incorporate a version of Oxford, have made a tryst to meet every midsummer's day at noon on a bench in the Botanic Gardens.

8. **The Old Schools Quadrangle** behind the Divinity School has grotesques on the top of the west side of the building, created in 2009 from designs by Oxfordshire schoolchildren. These include the lion, Aslan, from the Narnia stories; Three Men in a Boat, including the dog Montmorency, from Jerome K. Jerome's classic; Tweedledum and Tweedledee and the Dodo from *Alice's Adventures in Wonderland*, amongst others. Commissions of this type help promote the masonry skills of younger practitioners. Grotesques are carved figures on high points of buildings, often whimsical – they are known as gargoyles if they also act as a downpipe for rainwater.

9. **Theodor Geisel, aka Dr Seuss** (1904–1991), created characters like the Cat in the Hat (the book of which includes the characters Thing One and Thing Two), the Lorax and the Grinch, keeping children amused with their anarchic exploits. He was a postgraduate student at Lincoln College in the 1920s; it was whilst doodling in lectures that he developed skills which allowed him to illustrate his stories.

10. **John Buchan**, a Brasenose graduate, who also wrote *The Thrity-Nine Steps* in 1915. This was a popular adventure book whose main protagonist, Richard Hannay, is said to have been a favourite of Ian Fleming, the creator of James Bond, 007.

17

The Mighty Pen

Good reading habits set down in childhood will encourage adult readers. Oxford has been an incubator not only for children's literature but also adult literature and learning. It is not surprising that in a place where reading and literacy are held at a premium, many distinguished and groundbreaking writers have thrived. Poets and novelists alike have put pen to paper, often using Oxford as a setting for their stories. And why not? Oxford makes a perfect backdrop. I'm able to feature only ten of them, so apologies to the many who may feel overlooked!

1. Name the aesthete and playwright who studied at Magdalen College?

2. Which famous dictionary is curated in Oxford?

3. Which twentieth-century author wrote about *Bright Young Things*?

4. Which nineteenth-century character's visit to a fictional Oxford has disastrous consequences for him and his family?

5. Which fictional beauty caused all the Emperors' Heads to perspire?

6. Which female author was unimpressed with Oxford?

   a) Jane Austen
   b) Virginia Woolf
   c) Dorothy Parker
   d) Jeanette Winterson

7. Which twentieth-century Poet Laureate was at preparatory (primary/elementary) school in Oxford?

8. Which poet/playwright regularly stayed at the Crown Tavern, near Carfax?

9. Which of these fictional characters did not attend Oxford University?

   a) Bertie Wooster
   b) Jay Gatsby
   c) Indiana Jones
   d) Sir Leigh Teabing

10. Which Brasenose graduate won the 1983 Nobel Prize in Literature?

Chapter 17 Answers

1. **Oscar Wilde.** The prize-winning Classics student from Trinity College, Dublin, arrived in Oxford in 1874 aged 20 to read Greats (Latin & Greek). Like many, he enjoyed the freedom of living a flamboyant student life. His subsequent relationship with Lord Alfred Douglas led to a court case, brought by Douglas's father, the Marquess of Queensbury, and imprisonment for Wilde in Reading Gaol. Once released, his life and health deteriorated and he died in poverty and obscurity in Paris in 1900.

2. **The** *Oxford English Dictionary*, published by the Oxford University Press, monitors and records the development of the English language and its many various uses around the world. This ever-changing publication was first conceived in the 1850s, but the first printed edition was not produced until 1928. A second, twenty-volume, 21,728-page edition appeared in 1989. Work continues on the Third Edition, which will be an online resource only.

3. **Evelyn Waugh.** His novel *Vile Bodies* satirises English society between the wars, characterising various barely disguised friends and acquaintances on the way. Bryan Guinness and his wife Diana Mitford, who later married the British Fascist Sir Oswald Mosley, were central to this set. Waugh's 1945 novel, *Brideshead Revisited*, also touched on this world. Of his fictional Oxford undergraduates, Sebastian

Flyte and Anthony Blanche were at Christ Church but Ryder, Waugh's narrator, attended an unnamed college, possibly Waugh's own Hertford College. Socially ambitious Waugh aspired to have studied at the bigger and more fashionable Christ Church. The multi-layered book explores aristocracy and Anglo-Catholicism in England during the interwar years, drawing strongly on Waugh's own experiences and beliefs.

4. **Jude Fawley**, tragic hero in Thomas Hardy's 1895 novel *Jude the Obscure*, travels to Christminster (fictional Oxford) with his family and (spoiler alert!) hangs them all in a fit of despair.

5. **Zuleika Dobson**. Max Beerbohm's satirical 1911 novella sees the head-turningly beautiful Zuleika visiting her uncle in Oxford at fictional Judas College. All the undergraduates fall in love with her and, by the end of the story, drown themselves. This outcome is anticipated by the Emperors' Heads, a set of statues outside the Sheldonian, who observe the impact she is having on the undergraduates. The heads, now thirteen in number but originally fourteen, were carved when the Sheldonian opened in 1669 but, due to erosion, have been replaced twice, this last set carved by local sculptor Michael Black in the early 1970s. It's possible to see a small wren on the wreath on the head of the emperor by the Broad Street gate.

6. a) **Jane Austen** visited Oxford as a child in 1783 and was briefly tutored there. She remembered, 'dismal chapels, dusty libraries, and greasy halls'. Despite this, many of her male characters attended the university, as did her father and two brothers. Her mother had family links to academics at All Souls and Brasenose.

7. Sir **John Betjeman**. His time at the Dragon School was captured in his autobiographical poem 'Summoned By Bells'. This famously eccentric school has been known to make sure that all children can fully participate in football games by introducing a second ball. It is the *alma mater* of actors Emma Watson, Tom Hiddleston, Hugh Lawrie and Tom Hollander, and of London Metropolitan Police Commissioner Dame Cressida Dick, amongst others. John Betjeman studied at Magdalen College, was Poet Laureate from 1972–84 and also championed this country's Victorian architectural

heritage, having spearheaded the 1960s campaign to save St Pancras station in London.

8. **William Shakespeare**. He often stayed in the Crown Tavern, now part of the Golden Cross shopping arcade off Cornmarket, with his friend, the proprietor and vintner John Davenant, on his regular journeys from London to his birthplace in Stratford-upon-Avon, Warwickshire. Early performances of his play *Hamlet* may have taken place in the Crown Tavern's timbered yard. John Davenant's son William (1606-1668), who became a writer, was Shakespeare's godson. Some say Shakespeare was the boy's father.

9. **c) Indiana Jones**. This professor of archaeology was educated at Chicago University, and had tenure at Marshall College in Connecticut. Bertie Wooster, the creation of P.G. Wodehouse, won a Blue at rackets whilst studying at Magdalen College. Jay Gatsby, created by F. Scott Fitzgerald and referred to as being a Varsity man, only attended a short post-World War One programme at Trinity College, Oxford. For those who are not Da Vinci aficionados, Sir Leigh Teabing is the nemesis of the hero Robert Langdon; although they both share an interest in finding the Holy Grail.

10. **William Golding** (1911-1993). His 1954 book *Lord of the Flies* describes the survival and conflict of schoolboys on a deserted island. He taught at Maidstone Grammar School and Bishop Wordsworth's School, Salisbury, and also saw action in World War Two. These experiences provided him with insights into human behaviour which are explored in this novel.

18

Murder Most Foul!

Detective fiction is extremely popular and has inspired many TV series. Having an attractive backdrop makes it even more appealing, so Oxford-based detectives frequently feature in screen-based dramas. One of the most famous of recent years must surely be Inspector Morse, with the main character played with consummate skill by John Thaw. Not only are the thirty-three episodes in the ITV series well plotted and filmed, but they have also led to a sequel and a prequel being made, both also set in and around Oxford. So many Oxford visitors are interested in exploring the very ground on which these detectives walked. For a guide, this level of interest can be a challenge as physical continuity is not always uppermost on a location finder's radar; characters can set off from central Oxford to arrive home in notional North Oxford when in fact they are in Ealing, West London, and it's not unknown for characters to walk through a door in one college only to appear in the quad of another! Even so, it is fun to explore the city and find locations from the series.

1. Name the fictional county near Oxford which gives its name to a popular TV detective series.

2. What is the name of Inspector Morse's loyal but sometimes frustrated detective sergeant?

3. Which twentieth-century crime writer was born and died in Oxford?

4. Who had a cameo role in almost all thirty-three episodes of the *Inspector Morse* TV series?

5. Which college did Lord Peter Wimsey attend?

6. What was Inspector Morse's given name (spoiler alert!)?

7. Which character created by Dorothy L Sayers takes a rooftop stroll on the Radcliffe Camera?

8. Where did a famous TV detective (another spoiler alert!) suffer a fatal heart attack?

9. What is the family name of the actor who plays Sergeant Hathaway in the *Inspector Morse* sequel, *Lewis*?

   a) Redgrave
   b) Fox
   c) Cusack
   d) Irons

10. In which decade is the prequel to the *Inspector Morse* series mainly set?

   a) 1950s
   b) 1960s
   c) 1970s
   d) 1980s

Chapter 18 Answers

1. **Midsomer.** The long-running series, *Midsomer Murders*, with over 120 episodes to date, initially starred John Nettles as DCI Tom Barnaby. Now the job has gone to his fictional cousin, John Barnaby, played by Neil Dudgeon. Most of the episodes are set in a series of villages in this fictional county, but the action occasionally strays into Oxford itself. Nearby Oxfordshire towns such as Thame, Wallingford, Dorchester-on-Thames and Henley also feature in the series in various guises.

2. **Sergeant Robert 'Robbie' Lewis.** In Colin Dexter's thirteen novels, Lewis is Welsh and is older than Morse; in the TV series he is a younger man, from Newcastle. This character is a perfect foil to Inspector Morse. Lewis is not highly educated but often is the one who makes an observation which leads to the case being solved. The character is played by Kevin Whately.

3. **P.D. James** (1920–2014). Phyllis James's father did not believe in educating women, so his daughters did not go to universit, although, later in life, she was awarded an honorary fellowship of St Hilda's College. P.D. James's detective novels are much admired for their tight plots, fine characterisation and acute forensic detail. Her principal detective is Adam Dalgliesh, who is also a well-regarded poet.

4. **The author of the *Inspector Morse* novels, Cambridge-educated Colin Dexter.** He created the protagonists around

which the TV series is based, although there were more episodes than books. Dexter had written the first book as a challenge, having found nothing worthwhile to read on a wet Welsh holiday. He was a strong supporter of the TV adaptations, accepting some of the editorial changes. Dexter lived in North Oxford from 1966 until his death in 2017. There are plans to erect a statue in Summertown, North Oxford, near to where Dexter worked for the Oxford University GCE Examination Board.

5. **Balliol College** was chosen by Dorothy L. Sayers, the doyenne of interwar detective fiction, for her aristocratic and foppish, yet intelligent, detective Lord Peter Wimsey. On his notional 100th birthday, Balliol College accepted a portrait of their fictional alumnus.

6. **Endeavour.** He had a Quaker upbringing and his father also admired Captain Cook, who sailed his ship *Endeavour* to the South Seas and discovered Australia. In the episode 'Death Is Now My Neighbour', Morse gives a clue to his name (creator of the *Morse* series, Colin Dexter, was keen on crosswords) by pointing out that his name was all around Eve (an anagram of 'Endeavour'). The detectives' names, Morse and Lewis, were chosen by author Colin Dexter from crossword setters he admired, one of whom was Sir Jeremy Morse, former chairman of Lloyds Bank, and the other a Mrs B. Lewis.

7. **Harriet Vane**, the amateur female detective, studied at Shrewsbury College, which was modelled on Sayers's own college, Somerville. This is the location for *Gaudy Night*, Sayers' best-known novel about Harriet Vane and her eventual husband Lord Peter Wimsey, a fellow amateur detective. Vane would have found a kindred spirit in Katherine Rundell, a Fellow of All Souls College, who is a keen tightrope and roof walker, who regularly roams the rooftops of All Souls. Her children's novel *Rooftoppers* won the 2014 Waterstones Children's Book of the Year prize. Her academic interest is the seventeenth-century metaphysical poet, John Donne. She was inspired by *The Nightclimbers of Cambridge*, a legendary 1930s text.

8. **Lonsdale College**, otherwise known as Exeter College. Inspector Morse is walking through the front quad of the College when he collapses and subsequently dies in hospital. The final episode was based on Colin Dexter's last book about Inspector Morse, *The Remorseful Day*. The title is taken from

A.E. Housman's 1880 poem 'How Clear, How Lovely Bright'. Brasenose was also used on occasion as Lonsdale College in this thirty-three episode series which ran from 1987–2000

9. b) Fox. Laurence Fox is from a well-known acting dynasty. His father James Fox acted with Dirk Bogarde in the 1963 suspense drama *The Servant*, while his uncle, Edward, was the star of the 1970s thriller *The Day of the Jackal*. His cousins Freddie and Emilia, and his siblings Lydia and Jack, are also actors (Emilia stars in the TV drama *Silent Witness*).

10. b) Primarily 1960s. Most episodes of *Endeavour*, the prequel to the Inspector Morse series, take a topical theme of the time, including CND protests, organised crime, race relations and police corruption, among others. The part of the young Morse is played by Shaun Evans. He works alongside Jim Strange, a young but conventional uniformed policeman who will eventually become his superior in the *Inspector Morse* series. Endeavour's strongest influence is his boss, Chief Inspector Fred Thursday.

Stars in Their Eyes

The Oxford University Dramatic Society (OUDS) has provided early opportunities for many who have gone on to become household names. Sadly, gone are the days when students were able to spend much of their time acting, as academic demands now take precedence.

1. Which actor, who plays a key character in a series of films about wizards, was brought up in Oxford?

2. Where, near Oxford, might you bump into Lady Edith Crawley?

3. Which four of these well-known British actors studied at Oxford University?

    a) Imogen Stubbs
    b) Felicity Jones
    c) Judy Dench
    d) Rosamund Pike
    e) Eddie Redmayne
    f) Maggie Smith
    g) Vanessa Redgrave
    h) Benedict Cumberbatch
    i) Hugh Grant

4. Which 2017 science fiction/robot/action movie was partly filmed in Oxford?

5. Name the play about grammar school boys applying to Oxford and Cambridge?

6. Which character comes back to life in order to save the world in a 2017 movie partly filmed in Oxford?

7. Which musical film features a bicycle ride in the Oxfordshire countryside?

8. Which film uses part of the Bodleian Library as a sick bay?

9. What is special about Professor Charles Xavier?

10. Which combative duo of actors starred at the Oxford Playhouse in 1966?

Chapter 19 Answers

1. **Emma Watson**, who played the part of Hermione Granger, Harry Potter's school friend, was brought up in Oxford and educated at the Dragon School and Headington School for Girls when she was not away filming. Watson's early interest in acting was encouraged by her local Stagecoach Performing Arts School. It's said the film crew acknowledged her professionalism by calling her 'one shot Watson'. She is now a UN Women's Goodwill Ambassador and a Visiting Fellow at Lady Margaret Hall.

2. **Bampton** is the fictional village of Grantham, near Downton Abbey, whilst the historic farmstead Cogges Farm, near Witney, doubles as tenant farmer Tim Drewe's home on the Downton Estate. This is where Lady Edith arranges for her illegitimate daughter, Marigold, to be fostered. Victorian Gothic Highclere Castle, in nearby Hampshire, designed by Charles Barry in the 1840s whilst he was also rebuilding the Houses of Parliament in London, is the location of Downton Abbey itself, although the kitchen scenes are filmed on a set at Ealing Studios.

3. a) Imogen Stubbs, Exeter College; b) Felicity Jones and d) Rosamund Pike, both Wadham College; i) Hugh Grant, New College. As for the others, Maggie Smith was at Oxford High School and started her acting career at the Oxford Playhouse. Judy Dench went to London's RADA (Royal Academy of

Dramatic Art), Eddie Redmayne studied History at Cambridge, Vanessa Redgrave studied Acting at the Central School of Speech and Drama in London, and Benedict Cumberbatch studied Drama at Manchester University and at the LAMDA (London Academy of Music and Dramatic Art).

4. *Transformers: The Last Knight*. The survival of the Earth depends on the outcome of a battle between good and bad robots, although human intervention may tip the balance courtesy of inventor Cade Yeager (Mark Wahlberg), archivist Sir Edmund Burton (Sir Anthony Hopkins) and Professor Vivian Wembley (Laura Haddock). She, critically, is a descendent of the wizard Merlin, whose magic staff is required to save the world.

5. *The History Boys*, by Alan Bennett, became a film starring James Corden, Dominic Cooper and Richard Griffiths. It deals with the continuing issue of accessibility. Many colleges now run summer schools and foundation years to encourage bright state school students to apply to Oxford. In any event, the process is very competitive with the overall place to applicant ratio around 1:5. Bennett himself came from a modest background to read History at Exeter College in 1954.

6. **Nick Morton**, played by Tom Cruise in *The Mummy* (2017). Despite having been killed in an air crash, Morton comes back to life to prevent Ahmanet, a superhuman but betrayed Egyptian princess, from taking her revenge on the world for having been buried alive.

7. *Mamma Mia! Here We Go Again* stars Lily James and features ABBA songs including 'When I Kissed the Teacher'. This prequel to the original *Mamma Mia!* film tells of Donna's time studying at Oxford in the late 1970s, before she travels to the Greek Islands. The breakout dance sequence starts in New College's Hall and continues with a bicycle ride in the Oxfordshire countryside, ending up at the ruined nunnery at Godstow.

8. **The Divinity School** is used as the infirmary of Hogwarts School of Witchcraft and Wizardry in *Harry Potter and the Philosopher's Stone*. The mid-fifteenth-century Divinity School, which was used for lectures, debates and oral examinations, has a beautiful 1480s pendant fan vaulted ceiling by William Orchard, including 455 roof bosses of the coats of arms of the donors who financed the building. Duke

Humfrey's Library also features as the restricted section of Hogwarts School Library, which Harry visits in his invisibility cloak.

9. Charles Xavier, or Professor X, is one of the most powerful telepaths in the world, the leader of the X-Men and the founder of the Xavier School for Gifted Youngsters. James McAvoy plays this character in *X-Men: First Class* (2011) and is installed as a professor in the Sheldonian Theatre. This 1669 building was designed by Sir Christopher Wren and is where university ceremonies take place.

10. Richard Burton and Elizabeth Taylor, at the peak of their fame, starred in an Oxford University Dramatic Society production of Christopher Marlowe's *Doctor Faustus*. The play was directed by Professor Nevill Coghill, Burton's tutor at Exeter College, when he was on a 1943 short RAF scholarship. Coghill nurtured Burton's love of poetry and encouraged him to act. The proceeds (they took no fee) financed the Burton Taylor Studio, rehearsal rooms and studio space named after them.

20

All That Jazz

Choral music took up a fair amount of time during the early years of Oxford University's life. Religious observance, as manifested by sung services, was a core part of many of the lives of those studying in the city, many of whom were in holy orders. Now visitors to Oxford can choose between a very wide range of music. Walking around you will see posters advertising musical events across the city, many organised by and for students.

1. On what day would you hear singing near Magdalen College?

2. Which rock group had to fly back specially from the US to fulfil a booking at a May Ball in 1964?

3. Which saint is commemorated in a stained-glass window by Edward Burne-Jones in Christ Church Cathedral?

4. Which world-famous popular composer left Oxford after only one term?

5. Which composer wrote the music for the hit detective series *Inspector Morse*?

6. Which Oxford building is said to be the oldest music venue in Europe?

7. Which group played at the Carfax Assembly Rooms in February 1963?

    a) The Kinks
    b) The Who
    c) The Beatles
    d) The Ramones

8. Which German-born composer gave a concert in the Sheldonian Theatre in 1733?

9. Which virtuoso cellist was born in Oxford in 1945?

10. Which musician performed a new symphony whilst visiting Oxford in 1791?

Chapter 20 Answers

1. **1 May.** The Magdalen College Choir sings *Hymnus Eucharisticus* at 6 a.m. from the top of the 144ft-high, early-sixteenth-century College Bell Tower. May morning is popular with students, with some even swimming (illegally) in the nearby Cherwell River. Cardinal Thomas Wolsey, founder of Cardinal College, a precursor of Christ Church, studied at Magdalen in the late fifteenth century.

2. **The Rolling Stones.** This legendary rock band were not very well established when they played in the town hall in early 1964. They took a £100 booking to play at the Magdalen College Ball a few months later. They then hit the big time and had to fly back from a US tour to fulfil the booking.

3. **St Cecilia, the patron saint of music.** Edward Burne-Jones and William Morris met as students at Exeter College. This 1874 project was one of their many collaborations. Part of the second wave of Pre-Raphaelite painters, they were strongly influenced by Dante Gabriel Rossetti and by art critic John Ruskin.

4. **Andrew Lloyd Webber.** Both his parents were classical musicians, as is his cellist brother Julian, so having an ear for a good tune may not have got their attention. Lloyd Webber won a place to read History at Magdalen College in

1965 but dropped out that same year to team up with lyricist Tim Rice. They wrote a show for Colet Court – the junior department of St Paul's School in London – which became *Joseph and the Amazing Technicolour Dreamcoat*. The rest, as they say, is history. Lloyd Webber is considered the most commercially successful composer ever.

5. **Barrington Pheloung** (1954-2019). This Australian composed the distinctive theme music for the 1980s *Inspector Morse* TV series. Pheloung used the Morse code dot-dash-dot signifiers to spell out the name Morse (_ _ , _ _ _ , · _ · , · · ·, .) which provided the underlying pulse of the composition. Pheloung also worked on the music for the series sequel, *Lewis*, and its prequel, *Endeavour*.

6. **The Holywell Music Room.** Owned by Wadham College, concerts have taken place in this building since 1748. The college also owns the King's Arms pub. Other colleges also own pubs around the town. The Lamb & Flag on St Giles is owned by St John's College, which has had a bursary for students funded from profits from the pub. This was known as the Beer Bursary. The pub is no longer managed by St John's but there are plans for it to be run by a local community group.

7. **c) The Beatles.** It only cost 6*d* to see The Beatles play in the Carfax Assembly rooms in February 1963. They were about to hit the big time, as the studio album including *Please Please Me* was to enter the charts the following week. Falling Leaves was the local support band.

8. **George Frideric Handel.** He came to London in the early eighteenth century and joined the entourage of King George II. In 1733, Handel visited Oxford and premiered his oratorio, *Athalia*, at Christopher Wren's 1669 Sheldonian Theatre.

9. **Jacqueline du Pré.** By the time du Pré was 4 she was asking to learn the cello. Sadly her stellar career was cut short by the neurological disease, Multiple Sclerosis, which forced her to stop performing at the age of 26. She was married to the pianist and conductor Daniel Barenboim and died in 1987, aged 42. She is particularly well known for her rendering of Elgar's *Cello Concerto*.

10. **Joseph Haydn** conducted his *Symphony No. 92* in the Sheldonian Theatre in 1791 as part of his trip to Oxford to receive an honorary degree from the University. For this occasion, Haydn presented a symphony he had composed as part of a commission for the French Comte d'Ogny several years previously, but which had not yet been publicly performed.

21

The Artist's Eye

Not only have well-known artists studied at Oxford University's Ruskin School of Art, but also the colleges have many fine portraits of past alumni, heads of houses and dons hanging on their walls. There is also a drive to update these portrait collections to make them more relevant to modern sensibilities. In addition, sculpture abounds throughout the city.

1. Where in Oxford can you see the rooftop sculpture of a naked figure?

2. Which nineteenth-century painter captured a famous view of the High Street?

3. Where would you go in Oxford to enjoy contemporary art?

4. Where in Oxford can you see an original painting by William Holman Hunt?

5. Where in Oxford can you see a sculpture of a nineteenth-century Romantic poet?

6. Whose innovative Flemish stained-glass work can be seen in Christ Church Cathedral?

7. Where can you see Sir Joshua Reynolds's only work in stained glass?

8. Who designed the St Frideswide Window in Christ Church Cathedral?

9. Who was unsettled by Jacob Epstein's statue of Lazarus?

10. Which Oxford-based disability rights campaigner has been honoured by a 2017 portrait?

Chapter 21 Answers

1. On the top corner of the Exeter College building which houses Blackwell's Art & Poster Shop, where Broad Street meets Turl Street. The sculptor is Antony Gormley, who used his own body as a model for this 2009 work which is called *Another Time II*. It is part of a series of sculptures positioned around the world and linked to an earlier similar series called *Another Place*. This sculpture is 7ft tall, is made of iron and weighs half a tonne. On occasion it is dressed up by students.

2. **J.M.W. Turner.** As a young man, Turner travelled around England, sketching and drawing as he went. Many of these studies were worked up into paintings. His 1810 view of the High Street was saved from export in 2015 and is now in the Ashmolean Museum.

3. **Modern Art Oxford, set up by architect Trevor Green in 1965.** This gallery operates a dynamic contemporary exhibition programme from an old brewery in Pembroke Street.

4. **Keble College Chapel** houses *The Light of the World* by Pre-Raphaelite painter William Holman Hunt. The architect, William Butterfield, didn't include this painting in his holistic decorative scheme for the college chapel so it initially had to be housed in the library. Holman Hunt was unhappy

with limitations on access, so painted two further versions. One is now in St Paul's Cathedral, London, and one in the Manchester Art Gallery. The allegorical painting which suggests it is up to the individual to invite Jesus into their lives and not the other way around, shows Christ standing beside a recently opened overgrown doorway, with the weeds representing sins.

5. **University College**. Despite being sent down in 1811 for his self-proclaimed atheism, there is a marble monument depicting the drowned figure of Percy Bysshe Shelley in University College. The statue was given by Shelley's daughter-in-law, Lady Jane Shelley, in 1893, as the work by Edward Onslow Ford was too large for the Protestant Cemetery in Rome where Shelley's ashes are interred. The poet drowned in the Mediterranean in 1822. He was married at the time of his death to Mary Shelley (née Wollstonecraft), author of the novel *Frankenstein*.

6. **Bernard and Abraham van Linge**. These Flemish brothers worked in Oxford in the 1620s and 1630s and made windows using a novel vitreous-enamel painted glass technique which allowed for a much improved range of colour and artistic expression. Much of their work was destroyed during the Civil War in the 1640s, although some survives, including in Lincoln, Wadham, Balliol and University College chapels.

7. **The antechapel of New College** includes a 1778 west window designed by Sir Joshua Reynolds (1723-1792) and executed by Thomas Jervais. The shepherds in the nativity scene are self-portraits of the two artists. Reynolds was the

first President of the Royal Academy, founded in London in 1768 to promote British art. He himself favoured the Grand Style of portraiture which drew on classicism and the High Renaissance.

8. **Edward Burne-Jones**. This early 1858 stained-glass window in the Latin Chapel, retelling St Frideswide's life story, creates a popular backdrop to the reinstated shrine of Oxford's patron saint. It seems overly bright compared to later, more sophisticated work by Burne-Jones.

9. Russian leader **Nikita Krushchev** was unsettled when he saw this sculpture in 1956, on a visit to New College Chapel, saying it exemplified decadent Western art and would give him nightmares. Epstein has carved the figure with a striking expression which is said to indicate the crossover between life and death.

10. **Dr Marie Tidball**, a member of the Law faculty at Oxford and a prominent disability rights campaigner, was painted by Clementine St John Webster in 2017 as part of a series of paintings to explore inclusivity and diversity at the University of Oxford. These paintings have been displayed around Oxford to redress historic imbalance.

Strange but True

As you might imagine, in a place as unique as Oxford there are some pretty curious tales, anecdotes and events. Some of them are unsubstantiated, but others are genuine. I've chosen some of my favourites for this final part of our virtual quiz-led tour around Oxford.

1. Which college had a student who was saved from a wild boar?

2. Which college hosts an annual tortoise race?

3. When is the next Mallard Dinner?

4. How did medieval academics keep books safe?

5. Which Oxford train route has announcements in Mandarin?

6. Where did an Englishman first take to the skies?

7. Which college bought a whole house just to retrieve a door knocker?

8. To which college dinner might you bring a thimble?

9. Which Latvian-born polymath and philosopher was chatted up by Greta Garbo?

10. Which Oxford classicist and wit was an early fan of facial recognition?

Chapter 22 Answers

1. **The Queen's College** still commemorates the escape from death of a student who was attacked in Shotover Woods by a wild boar, whilst reading Aristotle. He shoved the book down the animal's throat, shouting '*Graecum est!*' (It's Greek!). The boar perished and the event is commemorated with a formal winter dinner complete with procession, including a boar's head and an accompanying carol. There is a carved grotesque of a boar's head on the west side of the Bodleian Library, near the Sheldonian Theatre.

2. **Corpus Christi** holds an annual Tortoise Fair, inaugurated in 1974. Corpus's own tortoise is suitably named after Bishop Fox, the college's 1517 founder. Hot competition is provided by other college tortoises. One of the fastest recent victors was Shelley, from Worcester College. Money raised goes to local charities.

3. **January 2101.** All Souls College holds a ceremony at the beginning of every century involving a mallard duck. One flew from the foundations in 1438, when the college was created by King Henry VI and Archbishop Chichele to commemorate those killed in the wars against France. A Fellow is selected as the Lord Mallard. He holds a mallard on a stick (now only a replica) and is processed around the college on a sedan chair whilst others sing the Mallard Song. All Souls College has no undergraduates and no graduates (although in practice

it normally has a handful of Prize and Visiting Fellows). Its members are said to include the finest minds in the country.

4. Before the advent of printing, precious hand-copied books and manuscripts were chained to the desks or bookcases in libraries. Damage from damp was avoided by having libraries on the first floor, with vaulted space below to allow free circulation of air. The early university only had a handful of books, so a gift from Henry V's brother, Duke Humfrey, of 281 books and manuscripts during the 1440s was very special.

5. The Chiltern Railways route from Marylebone to Oxford brings shoppers to the factory retail outlet at popular Bicester Village en route. Many shoppers come from mainland China, so the announcements on the train are in Mandarin as well as English.

6. Merton Fields, adjacent to Christ Church Meadow. On 4 October 1784, James Sadler, a local pastry chef and amateur scientist, took off from Merton Fields in a hot air balloon and travelled 6 miles to Woodeaton. The Montgolfier brothers had masterminded the first balloon flights in Paris in 1783, whilst an Italian, Vincenzo Lunardi, was the first person to fly in a balloon in England, in September 1784.

7. Brasenose College. A bronze door knocker from a building on this site was taken to Stamford in Lincolnshire in the fourteenth century by some dissenting students. In 1890, Brasenose College, founded in 1517, bought a house in Stamford called Brasenose House, to reclaim the door

knocker, which is now installed in the college hall. Ties worn on occassion by alumni of this college also bear this image.

8. **The Needle and Thread Dinner** at The Queen's College, when the bursar pins a needle and thread onto each attendee and exhorts them to be thrifty. The origin of the dinner derives from a pun on the name of the founder in 1341, Robert de Eglesfield. In French, *aiguille et fils* means 'needle and thread'.

9. **Isaiah Berlin** (1909–1997), not normally known for his looks, was complemented on his beautiful black eyes by Swedish film icon Greta Garbo. Berlin came to England as a child, taking first-class degrees in two subjects before focusing on philosophy and political thought. He was instrumental in the 1965 foundation of Wolfson College, a postgraduate college, and was its first president.

10. **Maurice Bowra**, classicist and wit, covered his face, not his genitals. when spotted by a passing woman at Parson's Pleasure, a popular nude bathing spot on the River Cherwell. 'I don't know about you, gentlemen,' he remarked to his fellow bathers who had done the opposite, 'but in Oxford, I, at least, am known by my face.' There is a fine, seated sculpture of Bowra by John Doubleday in the garden of Wadham College, where he was warden from 1938–70.